PICASSO

©1981 Ediciones Polígrafa, S. A.

Reproduction rights S.G.A.E. - SPADEM
Original text in Catalan
Translation by Kenneth Lyons

First published in the United States
of America in 1985 by:

RIZZOLI INTERNATIONAL PUBLICATIONS, INC.
597 Fifth Avenue/New York 10017

Library Congress Catalog Card Number: 85-42962
I.S.B.N.: 0-8478-0652-9

Printed in Spain by La Polígrafa, S. A.
Parets del Vallès (Barcelona)
Dep. Leg.: B. 15.744 - 1985

Josep Palau i Fabre

PICASSO

RIZZOLI
NEW YORK

FOREWORD

Art has at all times, since time began, been different: different in each country, in each nationality (or in each society), at each twist and turn in history.

In former times these changes were slower; they often came about so gradually, indeed, as to be almost imperceptible. The transition from Romanesque to Gothic, for instance, took place in a series of stages. And it was a change of direction in customs, in clothes, in ways of living (the move from castle to mansion is an example), together with a few discoveries, that brought Europe out of the Middle Ages into the Renaissance. Art has in all ages reflected the life of its time. Could one really expect, therefore, that the art of the twentieth century, after all the radical changes undergone by contemporary society, would continue to be what it had been? And yet the art of the Renaissance, with all its subsequent developments, down to and including Impressionism, had achieved such a strong position among us (perhaps because, at bottom, it flattered us) that it finally seemed to be the only possible kind of art; as though all man's strivings until so recently had crystallized once and for all in the rules laid down by this school or movement. How, I ask again, in an age when man is going through the most profound transformations he has known since the discovery of fire, can his art remain unalterable, unaffected by such a thoroughgoing upheaval?

I believe that this consideration is an essential one for anybody wishing to understand the profound mutation undergone by twentieth-century art, a mutation assumed and embodied by Picasso more than by any other artist. The trouble is that this time the evolution has not been gradual but sudden, syncopated, almost brutal. But then the changes in our customs and life-styles, and the scientific discoveries of our age, have taken place at a similarly dizzying speed.

If we are to understand Picasso's art and its scope properly, we must not forget these discoveries or inventions, some of which have meant (or still mean) veritable revolutions in our concepts of life.

Let us consider, for instance, the repercussions that the application of electricity has had: the lighting of our homes and streets, electric trams and trolley-buses, X-rays, ultraviolet rays... Let us recall that as long ago as 1838 the invention of photography had caused Delaroche to exclaim: "Painting is dead!" The invention of the cinema was just as important or more so. And then, in the nineteen-fifties, television became the public boon or pest we know so well. I have deliberately chosen to mention photography, cinema and television, three inventions which have helped to shape the optical sensibility of modern man and, therefore, have a very direct impact on the plastic arts. But there has also been a whole series of other inventions or discoveries, which may have had an indirect or transposed influence but are no less important.

5

Even though we may not realize it, their existence determines our way of thinking, filters through the cracks in our way of living and acting, and transforms our mental pictures and attitudes. In saying this I am thinking, above all, of relativity, psychoanalysis, astronautics and computer science.

There is one last factor in the conceptual renewal of our time, as decisive as any of the above or more so, and that is the ideological aspect. By this I mean the appearance of certain doctrines, especially anarchism and Marxism, which disturb the whole face of society and, whether accepted or rejected by that society, undoubtedly modify human relations, principally those confronting capital and labour.

The formation and the development of these social theories are inseparable from that all-important phenomenon, the industrial revolution; and the latter, in turn, is inextricably bound up with the resurgence of nationalities, some of which attained their freedom after the first World War, and others after the second — and there are many still struggling for their independence today. In order to link Picasso with Catalonia in our minds, without resorting either to clichés or to chauvinism, we need only recall that he was living in Barcelona when most of the socio-political transformations of the age in Spain (such as the loss of Cuba and the Philippines) took place, that he was well placed to appreciate the nineteenth-century revival of art and letters known as the Catalan "Renaissance", and that the industrial revolution had a much more decisive impact in Catalonia than anywhere else in the whole Iberian Peninsula. This last fact, indeed, made the region seem a thoroughly modern country in comparison with the rest of Spain.

STAGES

Pablo Ruiz Picasso, who in later life was to adopt, and impose on the world, his mother's surname of Picasso, was born in Malaga on 25 October 1881.

In this case, to my mind, being born in Malaga means particularly being born in Andalusia and among Andalusians, a people with very clearly defined characteristics, some of which we will see developing in the artist's work and personality. His parents' names were José Ruiz Blasco and María Picasso López. The father was a painter and drawing master, who taught at the Provincial School of Fine Arts in Malaga. One of his brothers, Salvador, was a doctor and chief of the health department of the port of Malaga, while another brother, Pablo, who had died three years earlier (and in memory of whom Picasso had been given the same Christian name), had been a canon of the cathedral. Through these three different worlds — the teachers at the Fine Arts School, the doctors of the State medical services and the ecclesiastical hierarchy — the boy Picasso very soon formed a tolerably exact knowledge of the inner workings of a very influential part of society, inasmuch as he was permitted to see all its machinations from the inside. This may well have left such a deep impression as to mark him for the rest of his life.

At the moment of birth Picasso was at first thought to be stillborn, until his uncle Salvador obtained a very lively reaction by blowing cigar smoke in his face. His parents later had two daughters: Lola, who was born in 1884, and Concepción, born in 1887.

Picasso also had two girl cousins, Carmen and María de la Paz, and since his parents' household also included his maternal grandmother, Doña Inés, and her daughters Eladia and Eliodora, and the family had a maidservant as well, little Pablo in his home circle was surrounded by a positive sea of skirts and petticoats. Whenever his father was absent, teaching at the School or attending to any personal business, it must almost have seemed to the child that he himself was the only male of the entire species. This, too, may have left indelible marks on his developing mental attitudes.

While the family were still living in Malaga, Picasso was photographed twice: once when he was four years old and a second time when he was seven, along with his sister Lola. Thus we can see that the possibility of representing the human figure by mechanical means was something of which he was made conscious at a very early age. Undoubtedly, too, his father must have talked to the other teachers and artists of Malaga about the scope of photography and whether it invalidated the art of portraiture or not. Among those teachers there was one in particular, Antonio Muñoz Degrain, who had a considerable reputation and for whom Don José Ruiz had a great admiration.

The Ruiz Picasso family lived precariously. Don José had two rather meagre salaries, as a drawing master and as curator of the Provincial Museum, but even between them they were barely enough to make both ends meet. Thus Picasso was accustomed from infancy to straitened circumstances, a situation that lasted through his childhood and early manhood. And although his own position improved when he was about twenty-four, the traces left by his family's poverty seem never to have disappeared completely. It was this material precariousness that finally obliged his father to apply for the post of drawing master at the Da Guarda Instituto (high school) in Corunna, which evidently assured him of a somewhat larger income. And so Don José moved to Corunna during the autumn of 1891, taking with him his wife and their three children.

The earliest drawings by Picasso still extant were done in Malaga in 1890, that is to say at the age of nine or ten (Fig. 2). There are also a couple of little pictures which are as old as, or older than, the drawings (Fig. 3).

Corunna, 1891

Corunna represents a fundamental chapter in Picasso's life. He arrived there just before his tenth birthday and left the city when he was thirteen and a half.

Picasso's childhood was profoundly conditioned by his father's psychological state. Don José, who was fifty-four when he made the move to Corunna, felt himself to have been in some measure defeated by life. He had wished, perhaps, to be a great artist, and he was simply a drawing master and a very mediocre academic painter. And then he had to maintain a household with six mouths to be fed, including the maidservant's. His wife was now thirty-seven years old and his children ten, seven and four. He himself was frequently ill or indisposed, and if anything happened to him he had no idea what might not become of that wife and those children. His only hope was that his first-born, Pablo, would soon grow up and be able to help the family — even to take his father's place if necessary. Children feel these tensions in the home much more intensely than their elders suspect. Don José only wanted his son to grow, to grow... And little Pablo himself wanted to grow and grow... Perhaps this feeling was to accompany him for the rest of his life. Perhaps it was one of those psychic effects that would never quite leave him.

During the first academic year in Corunna (1891-92), the boy was too young to be admitted to the Fine Arts School and could only attend the ordinary classes at the secondary school. But during the second, third and fourth academic years spent there (1892-93, 1893-94 and 1894-95 respectively), he was enrolled in several subjects at the Fine Arts School, where his own father was his only teacher. The situation was a little paradoxical, above all because the pupil already knew more than his master.

In the examinations at the end of the 1892-93 course, Picasso obtained first-class honours (*excelente*) with a certificate of merit. Why was he not likewise awarded this certificate of merit at the end of the other two courses, even though he obtained first-class honours again on both occasions? I certainly do not suppose that it was his father who grudged it to him. Is it possible that there was some other pupil who could compete with him on equal terms? It is rather difficult to believe this. Possibly, of course, the certificate of merit also brought with it some material or monetary reward, and the other teachers at the school considered that it was hardly fitting for the father to grant such certificates to his own son, even though Don José might argue that his son was head and shoulders above any of the other pupils — and equally superior to the father himself.

In support of this we do know that one day late in 1894 or early in 1895, Don José, who used to have his own pictures of doves — a subject he was very fond of painting — finished by his son, gave Pablo his palette, his colours and his paintbrushes, and never painted again. His son had grown a great deal, and very quickly. Perhaps even more quickly than the father had bargained for. This occurred when the boy was just thirteen; most probably, therefore, when he was undergoing the usual upsets of puberty. The fact that in later life his creative faculty always ran parallel to his erotic activity may well lead us to suppose that it was at this time that his sexuality first revealed itself.

We also know that in Corunna Picasso fell in love with a girl of about his own age. And this is a fact that should be given the importance it deserves. We far too frequently find adults indulging in either irony or false benevolence when they speak of "*les verts paradis des amours enfantins*", as Baudelaire calls them, and forgetting that the amatory capacity of a human being can be aroused most violently during childhood. Bearing in mind Picasso's precocity as an artist, it seems logical enough to suppose that a similarity precocity obtained in all the other aspects of his character; in that of sensitivity, for instance, and in that of the affections.

Another thing worth recording, in any case, is that in Corunna Picasso also saw death very close at hand, for it was the death of one of his own family. His younger sister, Concepción, had caught diphtheria and died of it on 10 January 1895, despite all the efforts made to save her by the family friend, Dr Pérez Costales.

All the events I have just related took place within a very short time of each other. And now Don José, who had gone to Corunna against his real inclination and was not happy living there, managed to obtain authorization to exchange posts with a Galician teacher then working in Barcelona. On this account he asked that his son should be permitted to take his examinations in advance, but was given this permission for only one subject.

Perhaps to retaliate in some measure for this rebuff, before leaving Corunna Don José organized an exhibition of pictures by his son in the room behind a shop in the city. This show probably included all the larger works which Picasso took with him to Barcelona: *Man in Beret* and *Old Galician,* now in the Picasso Museum in Barcelona, and *Beggar in a Cap* (Fig. 5) and *The Barefoot Girl,* both in the Picasso Museum in Paris.

By the time he left Corunna, Picasso was already an excellent draughtsman and a good painter. There is one surprising note in some of the paintings he did then, such as *Country Scene* (Fig. 6), and that is his use of light colours, so very much at variance with the prevailing academic concepts.

Picasso, with his parents and his sister Lola, now returned to Malaga; on their way they passed through Madrid, where they did not spend the night but did have time to visit the Prado. He spent the rest of that spring and a great part of the summer in his native city. One result of his stay is the *Old Fisherman* (Fig. 8). I can think of no other painter who ever painted a comparable work at the age of thirteen.

Barcelona, 1895

Barcelona!

There are only two names of cities in Picasso's life that can be written thus, with an exclamation mark: Barcelona and Paris.

Barcelona was to mean many things to Picasso, but I feel sure that he arrived there already disposed to like it, knowing that he was coming to a really modern city, which was even then expanding at a great rate. This, perhaps, was the first point in common he had with it, and possibly the most important: the city was growing and so was he.

Of all the numerous inventions and discoveries I have mentioned as important features of the twentieth century, some of the principal ones were to be first heard of by Picasso in Barcelona.

It was there that he first heard about anarchism and communism, though much more about the former than about the latter. And not as a theory, which might perhaps be put in practice (for he may have heard that before), but as a political practice based on theories, one that had quite a few followers and a profound effect on the life of the city. Only a few months after Picasso's arrival the famous bomb was thrown in the carrer de Canvis Nous, killing a number of people.

At the Escola de Belles Arts de la Llotja (the Stock Exchange Fine Arts School, at which his father enrolled him) he listened to his new classmates talking about *Modernisme* (the Catalan form of Art Nouveau), Symbolism, El Greco. They also argued about the new movement known as Impressionism, which two Catalan painters, Rusiñol and Casas, had brought home with them from a visit to Paris, and which had certainly influenced their painting, making them replace their browns with greys and causing the new movement to be described as the "revolution of the greys". Others, especially those working in Sitges, showed this influence much more openly: these were the "Luminists". And the new art of the poster also had many enthusiasts: Miquel Utrillo, Adrià Gual, Alexandre de Riquer... Then there was a group of very young painters, only recently graduated from the Llotja, who imitated the French Impressionists by going out into the open air to paint. Since many of them had to work at other jobs to earn their living, during the long summer evenings they would meet after work and go out together to the nearest really "country" place — Sant Martí de Provençals — to paint the sunset there. Since the dominant tones in these paintings would naturally be the yellows, these young artists were known as "the Sant Martí crowd" or "the saffron band".

One of the most important inventions of the age, electricity, was to expand so rapidly as to become a tangible feature of public and private life during the years Picasso spent in Barcelona. In the newspapers of the day we find constant references to this, for the novelty was really of the first importance. Just a few hours of an electricity cut today, with our lifts and household appliances paralysed, are enough to take us back to that sinister pre-electric world, dominated by shadows and blackness. Dark corners, dim corridors and bogy-filled "black rooms" have almost altogether disappeared from our houses. But Picasso was so accustomed to this fitful alternation between *chiaro* and *scuro* that for the rest of his life he was to paint quite as often by night as by day.

During the years 1899 and 1900 the Barcelona trams, hitherto drawn by horses, were replaced by electric ones.

There was one invention that Picasso was to experience for the first time in Barcelona, and that was the cinema. Two local photographers, the Fernàndez brothers, were very quick to bring this new marvel from Paris, where it had been presented by the Lumière brothers on 28 December 1895. Before the following year had ended — on 4 December 1896, to be precise — they gave their first showing at what was to be known as the "Cinematógrafo Napoleón". Picasso told me that he frequently went there, at first with Manuel Pallarès and later with the Reventós brothers.

There is another aspect of Picasso's early years in Barcelona that I feel should be emphasized. Until he arrived there all his travelling had been done with his parents. But from the moment they settled in Barcelona, although he still made an occasional journey in their company, he acquired the habit of travelling by himself, whether around the city or beyond its confines. His trip to Madrid in 1897 appears to have been made alone. And when he spent eight months in or around Horta d'Ebre in 1898, he went there with his host, Manuel Pallarès, but he returned alone, early in 1899. His visits to Sitges and Badalona, and the first trip to Paris, were made with his friend Casagemas. Thus Barcelona became for Picasso, not only his habitual residence but also the starting-point from which he set out on his great adventure. We should remember that when he visited Madrid he was only just sixteen years old. Yes, the city was growing, but he was growing too...

The first studio

His parents were wise enough to foster this independence of his, notably by renting a painter's studio — his first studio! — for him, at No. 4 in the carrer de la Plata, in 1896.

He was to have many other studios, whether in Barcelona (carrer d'Escudellers Blancs, Riera de Sant Joan, carrer Nou de les Rambles, carrer Comerç), in Paris or elsewhere; and he was to know other cinemas, and perhaps rather grander ones, a city with even brighter lights. But the mental attitudes with which he confronted them had been shaped in Barcelona.

As we have seen, Picasso was enrolled at the Stock Exchange Fine Arts School, the celebrated "Llotja", the principal of which at that time was Antoni Caba. To keep his father happy he attended the academic courses there as best he could and entered for official competitions: it was with this intention that he painted *The First Communion* in 1896 and *Science and Charity* in 1897 (Fig. 16). His father, still holding the old-fashioned idea of a painter as a servant of Court, Church or State, conceived the artist as a man intent on winning medals, receiving official commissions or working as a museum copyist. He appears to have ignored — or mistrusted — the life of the modern painter of his day, independent and Bohemian, and working for art dealers or for bourgeoisie, which in Barcelona was beginning to follow the example of its counterpart in Paris. Picasso soon discovered these new possibilities and, more independent than anybody else, did a lot of works on his own account which attempted to work out the most widely-varying pictorial solutions and were the result of his all-embracing spirit of innovation. Even at this early age each of Picasso's works adumbrated a new perspective, a fresh way of looking at things. Many of his pictures were of small dimensions, and many of them painted on wood, for at that time he could not afford to buy the materials he wanted. And yet some of the self-portraits he painted then are real masterpieces.

Madrid, 1897

The fact that he had been awarded an Honourable Mention for *Science and Charity* at the 1897 General Fine Arts Exhibition in Madrid was most probably what decided Picasso's father to send the boy to that city for the 1897-98 course, so that he could study under Muñoz Degrain. But Pablo soon rebelled against his official training and stopped attending his classes. Some beautiful colour studies that he painted in the Retiro Park in Madrid seem to reflect his own loneliness as much as, if not more than, that of the place depicted. Finally he caught scarlet fever and on his recovery returned to Barcelona, in June 1898.

Horta de Sant Joan

A few days after his return to Barcelona he left it again with his friend Pallarès for the latter's native place, the village of Horta de Sant Joan, where he stayed for eight months. While there the two friends spent some time living and painting in the open air, in the rugged mountain district known as the Ports (Passes) del Maestrat. In February 1899, when Picasso had quite regained his health and had finished the picture he intended to send to the next Fine Arts Exhibition, he returned to Barcelona. He was later to say: "Everything I know was learnt in the village of Horta." To my mind this phrase does not refer so much to any knowledge of painting as to human knowledge, to his discovery of a man's relationship with his lands and his beasts, as also to the old country crafts he had seen the local people practising, and to the friendliness and kindly atmosphere he had experienced in his friend's home.

The war in Cuba had ended while he was in Horta de Sant Joan. During the remainder of 1899 and part of 1900 his work reflected the dark mood that seemed to have infected all the young people of the time, after the disastrous loss of the Spanish colonies. This was the period of the *black Spain* depicted by Verhaeren.

The "4 Gats"

Picasso now began to frequent the *4 Gats* cabaret-cum-beerhouse, run by Pere Romeu, where Rusiñol, Casas and Miquel'Utrillo held sway and one could hear talk and argument on all the "-isms" of the day. Pablo soon made one of a circle of close friends who met there regularly: Casagemas, Sabartés, Vidal Ventosa, the brothers Àngel and Mateu F. de Soto, Sebastià Junyer-Vidal and a few more. At the *4 Gats* he also met and became friendly with all the Catalan artists of the time, including such figures as Mir, Nonell, González, Gargallo, Manolo, Pitxot, Torres García and others. It was here, too, that he held his first one-man show, in February 1900, a show that consisted largely of portraits of the friends he had made at the same establishment.

First visit to Paris

Picasso visited Paris for the first time in the autumn of 1900, in the company of Carles Casagemas; shortly after their arrival the two friends moved into a studio just vacated by Nonell, at No. 48 in the rue Gabrielle, where they were joined by Manuel Pallarès a few days later. During this visit Picasso made the acquaintance of Pere Manyac, a young Catalan art dealer living in Paris, who agreed to take the painter's entire output for a hundred and fifty francs a month. Now, too, Picasso painted *Le Moulin de la Galette,* at once a tribute and a challenge to Impressionism. The subject, Impressionist *par excellence,* is depicted in tones that suggest a *camera obscura.* While in Paris Casagemas fell head over heels in love with a girl called Germaine, one of the models they met there, and in an attempt to cure him of his infatuation Picasso took him home to Barcelona with him for Christmas, and then to Malaga for the New Year. But Casagemas left his friend there and returned to Paris, where he committed suicide.

"Arte Joven"

Picasso heard about Casagemas' suicide in Madrid, where he had gone in February and where he and another Catalan friend, F. d'A. Soler, founded the review *Arte Joven,* partly inspired by the ideas of the Catalan form of Art Nouveau known as *Modernisme.* He and Soler, in fact, performed the same functions in this review as did Casas and Utrillo, respectively, in the Barcelona review *Pèl & Ploma*. But the new review soon failed. Manyac was now urging Picasso to send him the works he had promised in order to organize an important exhibition at the Galerie Vollard in Paris. So the artist returned to Barcelona, where he spent barely a month, collected some of the works he had left there and went off to Paris again, with Jaume Andreu, while Miquel Utrillo organized a joint show of work by Picasso and Ramon Casas at the Sala Parés in Barcelona and wrote a very favourable article on the younger man in *Pèl & Ploma*. During his second stay in Madrid Picasso had mostly painted the two extremes of society in that city: the aristocracy and the down-and-outs.

Paris, 1901

In Paris on 24 June, and jointly with the Basque painter Iturrino, Picasso presented a total of sixty-five of his works; it was a very varied, almost disconcerting collection, both in subject-matter and in conception, but the prevailing mood was fauvist, with bold, thick brushwork and very bright colours. But this brilliant beginning was soon checked. The profits from sales at this show most probably went to Manyac and Vollard, while Picasso simply continued to receive his monthly sum. He was now sharing a flat with his dealer, at No. 130 *ter* in the Boulevard de Clichy. Once the euphoria of the first months and the fine weather had passed, his vexations began; Picasso withdrew into himself again and his work developed in accordance with his state of mind. In the early autumn he painted half a dozen pictures of characters dreamily abstracted from their surroundings, and in these pictures we can easily see a transposition of his own feelings. They are, however, magnificent works, which would alone suffice to prove the greatness of their painter.

The Blue Period

Later on, and most probably because he was influenced by the idea that he was living in the flat (No. 130 *ter* in the Boulevard de Clichy) in which Casagemas had been staying before his suicide, his work began to be invaded more and more by blue and the figure of Casagemas reappeared in his painting. A visit to the women's prison at Saint-Lazare served to complete his wretchedness and to determine the universe of poverty and suffering that was to be the centre of what is now famous as the Blue Period. Picasso had also broken with Manyac and now found himself quite alone, with no friend to turn to.

Begun in Paris, the Blue Period continued in Barcelona. Throughout 1902, indeed, Picasso's subject-matter referred almost exclusively to the wretchedness and loneliness of women. Another, rather short, visit to Paris in the autumn served merely to increase the artist's depression.

Barcelona, 1903-1904

In 1903 and the early months of 1904 Picasso remained in Barcelona, where the Blue Period reached its climax and he painted *Life* (Fig. 50), *Poor People on the Seashore* (Fig. 49), *The Procuress* and *The Madman* (Fig. 53), among many other works. After his studies of women, a series of poor people, forsaken children, enfeebled old men and cripples passed in turn across the stage of this blue theatre. Different explanations have been given for the monochrome quality of the Blue Period, which is indeed hardly ever exclusively blue, but rather blue allied with yellow and with green, or sometimes with mauve or red. In my opinion the influence of the silent cinema was decisive at this stage in Picasso's career; what we see here is the triumph of the surrounding atmosphere over the classic chiaroscuro and over the polychromy of Impressionism. In *Life* the scene represented in a rectangle, which was originally intended to be a canvas on an artist's easel, seems to confirm this view, as though it were a projection on a cinema screen. And if this setting was done in blue, rather than in green or in any other colour, it was because blue had always been the painter's favourite colour. We ned only look at some of the drawings of this period, done in pencil or charcoal but with the date written in blue, to understand that for Picasso the Blue Period was more than anything else the most inward-looking stage in his career. Perhaps it was the same inwardness that came to us through the silent cinema.

Paris, 1904

On 13 April 1904 Picasso set out for Paris once again, this time with Sebastià Junyer-Vidal, to settle there for good. He moved into one of the studios in a building that was later to become celebrated as the Bateau-Lavoir, in Montmartre, where his Blue Period continued to develop during the first few months. But now his life was changing. A couple of amorous adventures helped to make his work less tragic and to fill it with the ochre tones of autumn; at least until the beginning of 1905, when red, rose and salmon tones appeared in his painting and gave it a much pleasanter character, together with a change in subject-matter. Actors and strolling players, circus acrobats and equestriennes, now invaded his pictures, his drawings and his etchings. For he was a regular visitor to the Cirque Medrano in Montmartre, and he had a behind-the-scenes acquaintance with some of the characters he depicted; that is why his work presents them to us both during their performances and in private life.

From this moment on there is one very evident factor which should never be forgotten: Picasso's work always reflects his experiences; it is much more a diary as it were, and even an intimate diary, than a purely objective body of work. Bearing this in mind, we can see that the blue, which at times seems to be about to vanish from his palette, makes an unexpected reappearance, that pink advances or retreats according to the artist's prevailing optimism or pessimism, and that what we call the Blue and Rose Periods (though the latter is really blue-rose) are therefore not successive and irreversible but often simultaneous and even interacting: *Group of Acrobats* (Fig. 60), *Acrobat on a Ball* (Fig. 64), *The Tumblers, The Woman with a Fan* (Fig. 70).

In the spring of 1906 all these entertainers gave way to a subject-matter which, though apparently deriving from its predecessor, in fact included features that almost contradicted it: horses and naked boys, presented against landscapes that are practically deserts and with something of an epic spirit about them (Figs. 71 and 72). Picasso's work frequently seems anticipatory, as though painted in response to some sort of presentiment. The works I have just mentioned reveal the need he felt for renewal, his urgent desire to get out of Paris and commune with nature. The visit to Gósol, in the Catalan Pyrenees, was clearly imminent.

During the month of May 1906 Picasso, accompanied by Fernande Olivier, returned to Barcelona to visit his family and see some of his friends: Ramon and Cinto Reventós, Vidal Ventosa, Enric Casanovas and a few others. From Barcelona he then left for Gósol, where he and Fernande stayed for about three months. Gósol is an important milestone in Picasso's career, and one that should not be confused with the Rose Period, for the predominant tones of his painting there are those of ochre and the theatrical subjects disappear, though this does not make his output unitarian. Among the tendencies that appear in the work done at Gósol is one we might call telluric, as though the artist were attempting to wrest their secret from the awe-inspiring mountains that surrounded him — the Cadí chain to the north and the Pedraforca to the west — and transposing that strength into the faces he painted. But the dominant feeling is that of Mediterranean classicism, then at the height of its popularity in Catalonia, which Picasso must have heard discussed by his friends during the few days he spent in Barcelona. For a short time he appears to have wished to become the paladin of this tendency. Indeed, works like *Two Adolescents, The Toilette* (Fig. 73) and *Large Standing Nude* (Fig. 79) are almost unrivalled examples of this style.

Picasso's constantly questing spirit caused other seeds to germinate at Gósol, sometimes under the influence of El Greco (as in *The Peasants*), at other times moved by his preoccupation with structure, which led him to the threshold of Cubism.

But the revolution he was endeavouring to bring about was not to be accomplished until about ten months after his return to Paris. During those months his pencil, his brushes, his chisel were all trying out different solutions to the problem of plastic expression, like the reduction of the face to a mask as in his *Portrait of Gertrude Stein* (Fig. 80), the lavish use of blacks or the all-embracing concept of rhythm, which led him into abstraction. And, finally, the stay he had made at Gósol, in its most characteristic aspect, which was that of the adoration of beauty, now came to his aid; not, however, by serving or accepting that beauty, but by contradicting it, scoffing at it, destroying it. This

aesthetic revolution is embodied in *Les demoiselles d'Avignon* (Fig. 89). This work, based on memories of a brothel in the carrer d'Avinyó in Barcelona, is the greatest revulsive in the whole of modern art. It destroys the whole western idea of beauty, the Greco-Roman tradition of art. All the painter's friends disapproved of this new venture of his. And so it came about that, just as things were beginning to go better for him, he found himself alone again. But this did not deter him from going on with his purpose. Only one man accepted and understood, fortunately, the artist's temerity: the art-dealer and critic Daniel-Henry Kahnweiler.

For ten years — from 1907 to 1916 — Picasso was to be engaged on this new venture, which later came to be known as Cubism. *Les demoiselles d'Avignon* was not yet Cubism, though it did contain the latent possibilities of that movement. This picture, indeed, can be variously interpreted as a final explosion of Fauvism, a triumph of Expressionism or even a skirmishing sally into the realms of Futurism.

The great artists of the day, many of whom — like Van Dongen, Modigliani or Brancusi — had been irresistibly drawn to Paris, were quite aware that they were living in an age of change and that modern art required a new language. Picasso, with Cubism, found that language. During the rest of 1907 and part of 1908, indeed, his output reveals the progressive working-out of the signs and syntax of this language. The chronological boundaries of Cubism are rather difficult to establish, but it is evident that the ten-year period I have spoken of may be taken as representing this "working-out stage" of the new movement. For some writers on art true Cubism does not begin until 1910. Nor is there any great unanimity as to which painters may be properly classified as Cubists. Picasso, after travelling this road alone for nearly two years, made a rather sudden "convert" in the person of Braque; and in late 1911 or early 1912 the new movement was joined by Juan Gris and Fernand Léger. These four painters have always since then been regarded as the major Cubists, though a host of less well-known figures gradually came to be identified with the style: Metzinger, Gleizes, Lipchitz, Marcusis...

Cubism

In most of the manuals and treatises written about Cubism, sooner or later we come across the division between analytic and synthetic Cubism. This classification, though it does perhaps fit the two main stages in the work of Juan Gris (and it may even have been Gris who established it), certainly cannot be applied to Picasso, for some of the works he painted during his first ten years as a Cubist (the ones done at Horta de Sant Joan, for instance) seem to be already synthetic, whereas some of those belonging chronologically to the later stage are totally analytic. For Picasso always followed his own independent line, which makes it impossible to confine him to such an elementary classification.

After *The Young Ladies of the Carrer d'Avinyó* (it was André Salmon who gave it its definitive title of *Les demoiselles d'Avignon*), Picasso, much influenced from about that time onwards by black African art, continued to work along lines which seem to be rather expressionistic or negroid, until the influence of Cézanne, which can already be detected in *Les demoiselles d'Avignon,* again became predominant; and so he went through what we might describe as a "Cézannien" Cubism until this, in turn, was transformed, during his second visit to Horta de Sant Joan, into geometric Cubism.

Cadaqués

While it may appear that up to this point Picasso was principally concerned with working out a new language for the translation of reality, somewhere along this road he seems to have become interested in that language for its own sake, in the system of signs he had been building up, as though the means had become the end. This process, which culminated during his stay at Cadaqués in 1910, led his work into the absolute abstraction of paintings like *The Guitarist* (Fig. 96) and then very gradually, in 1911 and 1912, re-introduced some elements of reality. But from 1912 onwards Picasso's very characteristic need to feel his feet firmly on the ground, plus the fact that he had been so much "up in the air" during his preceding period, led to the apparition of the papers stuck to his canvases (*papiers collés*) and constructions (*assemblages*) composed of different materials (wood, cloth, iron...), which proliferated throughout 1913 and 1914. This was an extremely important stage in the history of modern art, for it meant a flagrant break with the canons of the Renaissance and academic art; it meant, therefore, a possibility of looking at the world with new eyes.

Some of these *papiers collés* have a freshness that brings to mind the unspoiled look of a child. These experiments were what brought him back to painting properly so called, but frequently the works were false collages, for the painter either creates the optical illusion of a collage or leaves us wondering whether what we see is painted or stuck on, as in the 1914 *Portrait of a Young Girl* (Fig. 107), for instance, or in some still lifes done the same year.

None of these developments or reactions was ever totally irreversible, nor can they be too categorically formulated; as though what Picasso wanted above all else was to show us his absolute freedom. It was this strong-minded attitude of freedom that enabled him, in 1917, to take the apparently retrograde step of returning to the figurative.

While all this was going on, there had also been substantial changes in the artist's private life. When he returned to Paris from Horta de Sant Joan in 1909, he left his studio in the Bateau-Lavoir and moved into one at No. 11 in the Boulevard de Clichy. His acquaintance with Gertrude Stein and her family, whom he had first met in 1906, had meant a considerable improvement in his financial circumstances and this move to a new home was one of the consequences. But in the autumn of 1911, on his return from Ceret, he broke with Fernande Olivier and began his relationship with Eva (Marcelle Humbert). It is difficult to say to how great an extent the innovation of the *papiers collés* is related to the presence of Eva in his life; on the other hand, it is quite clear that all the works done around that time and bearing the inscription "Ma Jolie" or "Jolie Eva" were inspired by her. Letters — frequently block capitals, as though they were printed — were also among the elements that Picasso and Braque introduced in their compositions. This change to a new mistress brought with it another move, this time from Montmartre to Montparnasse, first to the Boulevard Raspail and then to the rue Schoelcher — where Picasso took an apartment that might have been expected to bring bad luck, its windows overlooking a graveyard as they did. In the month of May 1913 Picasso's father died in Barcelona. The outbreak of the first World War found the painter at Avignon, where he was staying with Braque and his wife. Most of his French friends and associates — Braque, Derain, Salmon, Apollinaire — were mobilized. Picasso returned to a Paris that seemed strange to him. Max Jacob and Gargallo were among the few friends of his still there. Then Eva, who had been ill for some time, died at the end of 1915. The following year was a very lonely one for Picasso, and this is reflected in the sombre tones of many of his works. He spent Christmas and the New Year in Barcelona. Then he returned to Paris, only to leave it again for Rome in February, along with Cocteau, for he had been commissioned to do the costumes and décor for the latter's ballet, *Parade*.

The return to the figurative

It is far from easy to state exactly how far the events he had lately lived through and the temporary disappearance of his dealer, Kahnweiler (who was a German citizen), were determinant factors in Picasso's change of pictorial direction. We should not forget, of course, that even in the very heyday of Cubism he had done some figurative works, such as the *Italian Woman with Basket* in 1909, the *Catalan Woman* in 1911 or the portraits of Max Jacob and Vollard in 1915. Who can tell, indeed, whether Cubism did not also represent, to some extent, the chimera of creating a new language for a new world! When these illusions foundered with the violence of the war, Picasso must have felt freed from his former ties and ready to try something new. But there can be no doubt that the work he did for Diaghilev's Russian ballet company was what finally decided him to make this change. Nor should it be thought that his break with Cubism was absolute or anything like it, for he returned to that style whenever and however it suited him to do so, adding something new to it each time. In Picasso's eyes, in fact, Cubism had simply become yet another of his possibilities of expression.

The Russian ballet

This alternation of styles can be seen already in the ballet *Parade*, which had its first performance in Paris on 18 May 1917 — and was presented in Barcelona on 10 November of the same year. While the drop curtain was completely figurative, and many of the costumes were apparently quite conventional, those for the dancers playing the "managers" were constructed like a walking house of cards; as though Cubism had become humanized or, at least, anthropomorphic.

Thus figurative works were henceforth to alternate with Cubist ones, sometimes in an apparently dissociated way but on occasion tending to their mutual reinforcement. The drawings Picasso did at this time, which have been described as "Ingres-like", might also be regarded as the result of the refinement demanded by the asceticism of Cubism. But his line-drawing portraits of Stravinsky, Satie and Falla in 1920, and later those of Reverdy (1922) and Breton (1923), seem rather to be the culmination of the delight Picasso had taken in line throughout his career.

There is certainly no doubt that the visit to Italy and the work he did for the Russian ballet company had revived Picasso's interest in the characters of the *commedia dell'arte* — especially Harlequin — and, with them, in the liveliness of colour they represented.

More than anywhere else this can be seen in the two versions of *Three Musicians* (Fig. 114), painted in 1921, in which he appears to have solved not only the problem of blending Cubism and figurative art but also that other problem, which had become particularly thorny during the earlier stages of Cubism, of obtaining a flat space that would not contradict the two dimensions of the canvas. The *Three Musicians* are at once characters and decorative elements.

Contrasting with this bidimensional work, during the same period (1920-22) Picasso painted a series of massive figures which, rather than evoking the world of classical antiquity (though reminiscences of Pompeii do form as it were their background), assert themselves by a massive forcefulness that can only be described as gigantism. Their hands, too, are fleshy and bulky and all of these figures — among them *Seated Woman* (Fig. 113) and *Three Women at the Spring* (Fig. 116) — seem to demand sculpture rather than painting.

The analysis of this stylistic bifurcation, and the question of how the painter succeeded in producing the two styles simultaneously and yet differentiating between them so clearly and consciously, would demand a study that has not yet been made, one which might well provide us with some valuable clues to Picasso's creative processes — though in this case it might be a sort of conceptual, if not material, vivisection.

His artistic output during these years was accompanied by another series of events of a very positive kind in his private life, chief among which was, of course, his marriage to Olga Koklova, a dancer in the Russian ballet company. They were married in 1918 and their son, Paulo, was born in 1921. Picasso also had a new dealer, Leonce Rosemberg, and had moved to a new apartment in the rue La Boëtie.

Harlequin, as though making use of that devilish capacity for metamorphosis that is latent in his multicoloured diamond patches, was to make a great many appearances in the course of these years, beginning with the *Barcelona Harlequin* (Fig. 110) and going on through the Cubist harlequins of 1918 until the ones painted in 1923, the model for which was the Catalan painter Jacint Salvadó (Fig. 117). The three versions of this harlequin, too, each so very different from the other two, represent an element that might enable us to analyse in depth the mutations which constantly came about in Picasso's mind and sensibility. In the following year a portrait of his son Paulo, *Paulo as Harlequin* (Fig. 118), would seem to have closed this series for the time being. Painted in the same year (1924) we have some exceptionally sumptuous still lifes, in which there is a perfect blending of figuration and Cubism, volume and bidimensionality, sobriety and richness (Fig. 120).

One of the most important compositions of this period, the 1923 *Pipes of Pan*, is regarded as a sort of culmination of this moment of fullness and euphoria, and contrasts very clearly with the much more convulsive feeling to be found in some works painted in 1925: *The Dance* (Fig. 121), for instance, or *The Kiss*. The first of these, partly inspired by the death of the painter's friend Ramon Pitxot, may have its more distant explanation in the fact that during the celebrated banquet in honour of the Douanier Rousseau, which was held at Picasso's studio in the Bateau-Lavoir in 1908, Pitxot at a certain moment began a frenzied dance. But why these contorted gestures, this violence, at such a remove in time?

In any case both of these works seem to be forerunners of what was to be the most characteristic aspect of Picasso's output in 1926, for his work that year was in a nervous vein, concentrating largely on guitars constructed of rags, cords and nails, these last facing the viewer directly. The same aggressiveness is to be found in the faces of his characters, whose mouths look like sphincters or toothed sexes.

These deliberately repellent or glowering visions were to continue throughout 1927, 1928 and 1929, but they were also to be increasingly counterbalanced by works in a hedonistic spirit. This hedonism can certainly be sensed in the etchings done as illustrations to Balzac's *Le chef-d'œuvre inconnu*. Picasso's relationship with Olga had been gradually deteriorating when, in 1927, he met Marie-Thérèse Walter, a girl who brought a counterweight of youth and freshness, so to speak, into his life. From this moment on, Picasso led a sort of double life, both in his personal relationships and in his art. The increasingly important presence of Marie-Thérèse brought with it the revelation of a series of new plastic values, including particularly the practice of sculpture. The harmoniously rounded figure of his model obliged the artist to cultivate form more than ever. During the year 1931 alone he went from sculptures in wrought iron, some of which were very aggressive, to the creation of very stylized figures carved in fir or pine, in which he seems to have been playing with the very fragility of his material. Finally, however, the forcefulness of the model's forms asserted itself absolutely in 1932 and 1933, both in painting and in sculpture. This is the period I have christened "curvism". In a comparatively short time Picasso created not only a series of paintings of great charm and liveliness, but also a number of sculptures that are among the most successful and innovatory in his whole career. The sense of monumentality was achieved without a monument and became an inherent part of the sculpture itself, which seems to look at us from a view-point corresponding rather to space than to time. It is indeed a distance of centuries.

Surrealism

Having reached this point, some reference must be made to Picasso's contacts with Surrealism. In my opinion Picasso's work in this direction began before what is officially known as Surrealism, which is usually regarded as having started in 1924. I am quite convinced that such a work as *Three Bathers*, painted at Juan-les-Pins in June 1940, is a definite antecedent of the movement. French Surrealism, that movement led by such men as Breton, Aragon and Eluard which was an irruption of irrationality in the possibly over-rationalized world of French culture, coincided at this moment with works like those of Picasso, who had never neglected the instinctive, fathomless aspect of painting. Needless to say, *The Dance*, which I have already mentioned, was hailed by the Surrealists almost as though it were their own creation. And in *Bathers with a Beach Ball* (Fig. 125), painted in 1932, the postulates defended by the group seem to be altogether attained.

At all events Picasso was then asked to do the cover for the review *Minotaure*, which was edited by André Breton, and this seemed to formalize a sort of circumstantial, temporary adhesion to the Surrealist movement. But then Picasso took possession of the figure of the Minotaur, which was not new in his work anyway, and made it altogether his own. Or, rather, he used the Minotaur as a pretext for narrating in coded language, through drawings, engravings and paintings, many episodes in his own life.

The *Suite Vollard* is a series of a hundred engravings which is made up of several sub-series, such as *The Sculptor's Studio, Minotaur* and *Blind Minotaur*. The hedonism that breathes through his illustrations for *Le chef-d'œuvre inconnu* is found here again, but even more intensely. Picasso, who with his Blue Period had shown the world that he had penetrated to the innermost essence of Christianity, perhaps for that very reason now decided to prove that he was also capable of capturing the essence of what we have grown accustomed to calling paganism.

This sort of personal confession through his work was to be the most striking aspect of his output for the next few years, culminating in the great

1935 etching *Minotauromachy*, in which all the symbols of the moment — horse, bull, raped woman, indifferent onlookers — were brought together. The elements of traditional Mediterranean mythology had become elements in Picasso's own mythology.

Also done in 1935 are a number of paintings, the best-known of which is called *The Muse*, in which softness and nervous strain, dream and reality, seem to be at odds once again.

It was at this point in his life that the Spanish Civil War began. His position was clearly defined from the very first moment, but Picasso knew himself, knew the forces that could be unleashed in him when he was driven by passion, and attempted at first to stick to a position of mockery and satire; until the bombing of the little Basque town of Guernica really aroused his rage, not exactly because it was a martial or political event, but because he was outraged at the thought of an immensely powerful force like that of the German air arm carrying out such a ruthless attack on a small, defenceless village. This moral detonator gave him his theme for the great frieze or mural that he had to paint for the Spanish Pavilion at the Paris International Exhibition in 1937. The bombing had taken place on 26 April and on 1 May he began to draw his initial sketches, some of which attained a pathetic quality such as he had perhaps never reached before (Fig. 126). Here we have passed from farce to tragedy.

Guernica

The first feature to be remarked in the working-out process of *Guernica* is the struggle that took place in Picasso's mind over whether or not to incorporate the symbols of his own personal universe in his great composition, and this struggle is evident in most of the preliminary sketches. Finally, however, he realized that he had to put aside any kind of untransferable or private subjective content and make an attempt to objectivize the great catastrophe. And *Guernica* is that: a balance between overflowing passion, which almost seems to be preventing us from seeing the picture, and the taming of these impulses, the serene vision which rises above the convulsion and succeeds in depicting it with perfect, balanced architecture (Fig. 126).

In the configuration of *Guernica* the artist has not, apparently, created any new style, as he had so often done before in the course of his career. But his whole past as a painter seems suddenly to rise up before his eyes and come to his aid. In the picture we can trace something of almost all his previous stages or periods — Realism, the Blue Period, Cubism, Surrealism, Expressionism, etc. — and they are all mysteriously bound together by a strange force that unites them, a stormy wind that crosses the mural from right to left and gives it the quality of an epic painting, one that is unique in Picasso's work and perhaps in the whole of modern art. That is how this picture, based on a specific event, became a cry that reached the whole world against the horrors of war. In this prospecting of his pictorial past Picasso had gone back to the very roots of his being and had, though perhaps unwittingly, succeeded in making the picture reflect his Andalusian substratum.

The consequences of the cry uttered in *Guernica* were to last for a long time — right through 1938 and 1939 — and were to lead, in fact, to the works Picasso painted during the second World War. It was from this point onwards that the human figure was to be presented in distortion, with its eyes out of their sockets, so far out that they finally come to be placed in some other part of the face, because weeping has made such a parody of the nose, mouth and other features of the human face that that face has become something inhuman, has become a sort of monstrous map of our five senses. This violent metamorphosis is perceptible in *Weeping Woman* (fig. 128), in which all the colours that in *Guernica* — based on strict black and white — had remained captive in the painter's tubes now shot all over the canvas, each trying to shout louder than any of the others. This loudness of colour and these infrahuman faces were to be the predominant features of Picasso's painting in the long, dark years from 1939 to 1944, during which he found a new model, one more in accord with the drama all around him. This new model was Dora Maar.

Some works, however, stand out from the rest or for one reason or another break away from the general rule, and the first of these is *Women at Their Toilette* (Fig. 129), done in the spring of 1938, just a year after *Guernica*. This is a picture which can to some extent be regarded as a counterweight or compensation, not only on account of its considerable dimensions, but also because it is almost altogether constructed of papers stuck to the canvas and because the colours, vivid and delightful, hit us right between the eyes and are clearly intended to serve a lyrical, intimist subject-matter. *Women at Their Toilette* may be described as the romping of a genius.

The second World War

Woman Dressing Her Hair (Fig. 130), on the other hand, which was painted at Royan in June 1940, shows us that the painter's vision has once more been marked by violence unleashed.

Synthesizing the work of Picasso always means betraying it a little, for it entails eliminating some of the facets that constitute its overflowing abundance and richness. But if I were obliged to choose the most representative works he did during the last two years of the second World War, I would choose two aspects which appear above all in his sculpture. In 1942, on the occasion of Juli González's death, Picasso painted a picture presided over by a bull's skull, but during 1943 he sculpted two skulls of overwhelming force and simplicity. One might perhaps even say that these skulls are possessed of life. But of what life? That of death or that of sculpture? That same year, at all events, the artist did several drawings of a man with a sheep, drawings which culminated, in the following year (1944), in the great sculpture known as *Man with Sheep* (Fig. 133). At the precise moment when it was created, the force of the sheep struggling to escape and the force of the man holding it firmly made this sculpture look like a symbol of life and hope. Even the man's attenuated legs seem to tell us that, despite his privations, despite his enfeeblement, he is still strong and vigorous enough to resist the pulling of the animal.

As though formally to close the period of the war properly so called, there is a picture called *The Charnel House* which was painted in various stages during the year 1945. This picture is unfinished, and the real reason for this checking of its flow should be sought in the very vitalism of the painter, which thus reveals one of his ways of working. On the one hand he wished to pay homage to all those who had died in concentration camps, but on the other he felt the need to forget the horrors of the war, the hunger and the cold, and to sing of life once again. This second feeling is the one that seems to prevail, perhaps because he himself had returned from death to life. In any case, by leaving the work unfinished his testimony is all the more trustworthy: he knew that he could not add another line, another brushstroke, artificially. That is one of the great lessons of his work. A rather similar judgment may be applied to his composition *To the Spaniards Who Died for France,* which was painted the same year.

The peace

Life now seemed to explode all over again for Picasso with an irresistible force, often through a new woman's image, that of Françoise, which he idealized until it became one of the star faces of his whole work. Life, indeed, exploded for him through painting, through lithography — the eleven variations on the figure of a bull seem to have sprung from the very depths of the earth and from some immemorial time, long before Altamira or Lascaux (Fig. 132) — but above all through pottery. In 1946 Picasso first tried his hand at this craft, at Vallauris in Provence, but it was not until the following year, in view of the encouraging results, that he grew bolder and, without ceasing to draw, paint or engrave, gave himself up to this new form of expression with all his usual enthusiasm. Plates, jugs, doves, reliefs, tiles, all much closer to folk art than to refined art, were the most characteristic results of his truly prodigal output, which also included some remarkable images of bulls. Psychologically this period, which also saw the births of his children Claude (1947) and Paloma (1949), is best represented by the picture *The Joy of Living* in the Picasso Museum at Antibes.

During the nineteen-fifties Picasso created a rather unusual form of sculpture constructed out of thrown-away things, which he collected as though they were treasures. He had already tried this form of expression to some extent when he constructed the head of a bull out of the saddle and handlebars of a bicycle in 1943, but now the works were more complex: *The Goat* (1950), *The Monkey* (1951), *The Thrush* (1952). That there is great ingenuity in these works is undeniable, but we should be falling into serious error if the existence of this ingenuity, which is so akin to the inventiveness and cunning of the Greeks in their best period, were to prevent us from seeing the wealth of plastic solutions it implied.

War and Peace

In 1952 Picasso synthesized the double experience undergone during the last fifteen years in two huge panels entitled *War and Peace* for a Romanesque church at Vallauris.

Disagreements with Françoise now brought this chapter of his work and his life to an end. But during the summer of 1954 the figure of Jacqueline began to take ever more definitive shape.

Undoubtedly the most important work Picasso did during the sentimental "interregnum" of the end of 1953 and the first half of 1954 was the portraits of Sylvette, the girl with the pony-tail that was then so fashionable. Through the youth of his model — Sylvette was about twenty years old — he rejuvenated his painting. The girl is seen from a different pictorial angle every time. That delight in variations and metamorphoses that Picasso had always shown through drawing and engraving was now extended to painting and was the beginning, I believe, of the new stage in the art. But now, instead of taking a living model as his starting-point, as in the portraits of Sylvette, he first combined an artistic model (Delacroix) with living models in *Women of Algiers* (1955). After that he did the variations on the interior of the house he was living in then, "La Californie". It was in *The Studio in Cannes* (Fig. 138), painted in 1956, that he attempted to give a soul to some rooms which had been left deserted and therefore dispossessed, soulless. Some of these rooms underline the emptiness that inhabits them; in others a rather small silhouette endeavours to integrate

The Maids of Honour

with the space and the furniture, to harmonize with them. As from the summer of 1957 the variations were effected, apparently, through an existing work of art, Velázquez's *Maids of Honour* (Figs. 139 to 144). It was to be an arduous task, for it was as though Picasso were attempting to hide from himself and us his true preoccupations behind the screen of purely pictorial concerns. His *Maids of Honour* are akin to those of Velázquez, not so much in the theme, the composition or the colour (in which they could hardly resemble them less) as in the endeavour to translate through painting coldly — and therefore to hide — his feelings, his states of mind. The struggle can be seen in the brusqueness of the line, the dryness of the brushwork, the aridity of some of the figures or compositions; until the great truth — not precisely that of the open windows, through which the painter has also eschewed confession — bursts upon us in the last two figures, in whom we see Jacqueline and a little maid of honour charmingly curtsying as she takes leave of the company.

In the spring of that same year Picasso came home one evening from a bullfight at Arles, shut himself up in his studio and, according to David Douglas Duncan, in three hours produced the twenty-seven dynamic aquatints of *La tauromaquia,* later published by Gustau Gili.

In 1958 he bought the Château de Vauvenargues, moved into it the following year and worked there for several months. The problem of the *home,* which we have already seen expressed through *The Studio in Cannes,* becomes very evident in these changes of abode. In the spring of 1961, however, he settled down for good in the old manor-house of "Notre-Dame-de-Vie", near Mougins in Provence.

Picasso was to continue concealing a large proportion of his secrets from us by transposing them through the interpretation of other works of art, as in the version he did in 1960-61 of *Luncheon on the Grass* (Fig. 146). Here, as in the cases mentioned above, I believe that it is not so much a question of a confrontation with the masters of the past — the view usually taken — as of a prextext to go on painting without the need to reveal his inmost thoughts to us, as was habitual in him. These inmost thoughts will have to be discovered, translated or sought by other means. We are dealing with a cryptic language.

With *The Painter and His Model* (1962-63), a constant theme in his work as it is in the history of art in general, much the same sort of thing occurs. The painter is Picasso, we either know it or suppose it. But who is the model? Is it always the same one? And is she the one *the painter* sees or the one he, Picasso, sees?

I have said that this wish to conceal himself was partial, because during these years drawing and engraving were to become increasingly important and they would frequently tell us what the painting hid from us.

With Jacqueline now permanently established in his life, Picasso began in 1961 (though he had tried his hand at it sporadically a short time before) an art form that was new to him: linocuts. Of this, too, he made a splendid art, which reached its highest point in 1962, though he continued to use the form for a few years longer. In most of these linocuts, perhaps because of the pleasure of the discovery, he created an objective art, or at least one of the most objective of his career. The colours are almost always explosive. As for the technique and procedure, one would say that they helped him to find an extrovert art, and that he himself finally used to provoke this result. In colour his works in this form were pure light and in this regard his linocuts may be considered eminently Mediterranean works. The sombre shadows that had invaded his life now seem to have been dissipated.

From 1965 onwards, after having undergone a major operation, and also after the great homage organized in Paris in 1966 to celebrate his eighty-fifth birthday, Picasso's life was to become a race against the clock — not to recover the time he might have lost, for he had never wasted time in his life, but to enter more deeply into the future or, to put it more clearly, to engage in a last struggle against death. His whole life, of course, had been just this sort of struggle, but now the fight was out in the open.

The last years
Between 1967 and the early months of 1973 Picasso's inventiveness and output, which had always been abundant, became a matter of overflowing prodigality: drawing, engraving, ceramics, painting and even sculpture were all practised almost simultaneously. It is evident that he still had many things to say, things that we would have to *listen to* and *read* in the years to come. For if in the course of his life his contemporaries had not had time to discover all the winding ways of his work, the work he was doing now was to leave so many doors open and so many question marks that it would be useless to attempt to expound them all at once. And in all these works there is one outstanding feature, and that is his freedom. Though it had never failed him in younger days, it now seemed more all-embracing than ever. Both in drawings and in engravings he mixed the most varied techniques and procedures. Coloured pencils and water-colour, characters of past and present, realistic scenes and chimerical visions in the drawings. Dry-point, etching, aquatint, burin, scraping, in the engravings. In both of these media, as also in the paintings that were shown at his two exhibitions in the Palace of the Popes at Avignon (1970 and 1973), we seem to see an explosion of some of the feelings that had been stifled in his earlier series of pictures, and which perhaps on that account now appeared with greater violence than before. The freedom was total, technical and conceptual. Eroticism, which had been one of his greatest sources of inspiration, now returned with unusual vigour. Celestina, that famous figure of a procuress from the classic Spanish theatre whom he had depicted during his youth in Barcelona, would seem to have been following in his footsteps and to have gradually grown old along with him, just as some of the harlequins of younger days — now old, too, and toothless — came back to him too. Along with all these picaresque figures and a string of rather shady or truculent characters, including bullfighters, Catalan peasants with their Phrygian caps and "dirty old men", we find the metaphysical visions — theatre within a theatre, characters with their doubles, a proliferation of faces — and some self-portraits, sometimes intentional and sometimes involuntary, in the most moving of which Picasso, looking himself up and down, examines in his face his own death. This death came to him on 8 April 1973.

Barcelona, January 1981
Centenary year of Picasso's birth

CHRONOLOGY

1881. Birth of Picasso in Malaga on October 25. In 1885 his sister Lola is born; and in 1887, his sister Concepción.

1891. September: the Picasso family moves to Corunna.

1895. Death of Concepción. Drawings and paintings: *Beggar in a Cap, The Barefoot Girl.* Exhibition in the back room of a shop.
Summer in Malaga.
September: the family moves to Barcelona. Picasso enters the Exchange School of Fine Arts, at which his father teaches drawing.

1896. *The First Communion,* shown at the Barcelona Fine Arts Exhibition.
Academic and free works. Self-portraits. Acquires a studio at No. 4 in the carrer de la Plata, but lives with his family at No. 3, carrer de la Mercè.

1897. *Science and Charity* is awarded an Honorable Mention at the Madrid Fine Arts exhibition. Foundation of the ''4 Gats''.
Autumn: moves to Madrid. Studies at the Academy of San Fernando and in the Prado.

1898. Returns to Barcelona in the spring. Spends the summer with Manuel Pallarès at Horta d'Ebre, most of the time in a cave in the ''Ports'' or Passes of the Maestrat range of mountains. Self-portraits. ''Everithing I know, I learnt in Horta d'Ebre.'' End of the Cuban War.

1899. Returns to Barcelona. Attends drawing classes at the Cercle Artístic. Acquires a studio in the carrer d'Escudellers Blancs. *Portrait of Josep Cardona.* Meets Sabartés. *Lola behind a Window.*

1900. Shares a studio with Carles Casagemas at No. 17 in the Riera de Sant Joan. February: exhibits at the ''4 Gats''. Many portraits: Soto, Sabartés, Reventós, Vidal Ventosa, Pitxot, etc. October: first visit to Paris, with Casagemas. *Le Moulin de la Galette.* Signs a contract with Pere Manyac. Christmas in Barcelona.

1901. New Year in Malaga.
February: journey to Madrid. Founds the review *Arte Joven* with F. d'A. Soler.
May: passes through Barcelona.
June: second visit to Paris, with Jaume Andreu.
Exhibition at the Galerie Vollard. ''Pre-fauvisme''. Meets Max Jacob. *Harlequin Leaning on the Table.* Breaks with Manyac. Beginning of the Blue Period. *Large Blue Self-portrait.*

1902. January: returns to Barcelona. Takes a studio in the carrer Nou, with Rocarol. *Drunk Woman Sleeping* (or *The Absinthe Drinker*), *Whores in a Bar.* Autumn: third visit to Paris, with Rocarol. Stays at the Hôtel du Maroc, suffering cold and hunger.

1903. January: returns to Barcelona, and to his studio in the Riera de Sant Joan. *Life, Poor People on the Seashore.* Autumn: moves to a studio at No. 28 in the carrer Comerç.

1904. Blue portraits.
April: moves to Paris with S. Junyer-Vidal.
Moves into the ''Bateau-Lavoir''. Meets Fernande Olivier. *The Couple, The Frugal Repast* (etching), *Woman with the Raven.*

1905. Blue-rose or Rose Period: *Acrobat on a Ball.*
Summer: visits Holland. *The Three Dutchwomen. The Tumblers, Woman with a Fan.*

1906. *Arcady.*
Gósol: *The Harem, The Toilette, Three Nudes.*
Paris: *Portrait of Gertrude Stein.*

1907. Spring: *Les demoiselles d'Avignon.* ''Primitive'' expressionism and pre-cubism.

1908. Cubism. Sojourn in rue des Bois.

1909. Summer: Horta d'Ebre. Geometric cubism: *Portrait of Fernande.*
Paris: *Portrait of Vollard.*

1910. *Portrait of Uhde, Portrait of Kahnweiler.*
Summer in Cadaqués. Abstract cubism: *The Guitarist.*

1911. Baroque cubism. Summer in Ceret.
Autumn: breaks with Fernande.

1912. First collage: *Still Life with Chair Caning.*
Spring-summer: Ceret and Sorgues.

1913. Beginning of the relationship with Eva. *Ma jolie, Jolie Eva. Ceret* (collage).
Autumn: *Woman in an Armchair.*

1914. Sojourn in Avignon, with Braque and Derain, when war is declared. Returns to Paris.
Pointilliste cubism.
Flat cubism.

1916. Beginning of his friendship with Cocteau. Realist portraits of Vollard and Max Jacob. Death of Eva.

1917. Visits Italy with Cocteau.
Paris: first performance of the ballet *Parade.*
Long stay in Barcelona: *The Barcelona Harlequin.*

1918. Marries Olga Koklova.

1919. First representational cubism: *Table Before the Window,* at Saint-Raphaël.

1921. Second representational cubism: *Three Musicians.*
Sojourn at Fontainebleau. Birth of his son Paulo. Neoclassicism and gigantism. *Women at the Spring.* Maternities.

1924. Aestheticist cubism: large still lifes.

1925. *The Dance.*

1927. Beginning of the relationship with Marie-Thérèse. Etchings to illustrate Balzac's *Le chef-d'œuvre inconnu.*

1928. Painted visceral sculptures. Abstract sculptures. Summer: Dionysia paroxysm of Dinard.

1932. Curvism: *The Dream.* Figurative sculptures: *Head of Marie-Thérèse.*

1933. *The Sculptor's Studio,* etchings for the ''Suite Vollard''.

1935. *Minotauromachy* (etching). Birth of Maia.

1936. Beginning of the relationship with Dora Maar.

1937. *Guernica.*

1938. *Woman with Cock.*

1939. *Night Fishing at Antibes.*
Autumn: Misshapen or distorted figures from Royan. Self-portraits.

1940. Monsters: *Nude Dressing Her Hair.*

1941-1943. Misshapen or distorted figures in Paris: *Woman in an Armchair.*

1944. *Aubade.* Sculptures: *Death's-head, Man with Sheep.*

1946. Antibes, with Françoise Gilot. *Woman-flower. The Joy of Living.* Ceramics at Vallauris. Series of lithographs.

1947. Birth of Claude.

1949. Birth of Paloma. Peace Congress.
Prolific creative activity: ceramics, drawings, paintings, engravings.

1950. Sculptures made with rubbish; *The Goat, The Monkey* (1952).

1951. Beginning of the relationship with Geneviève Laporte.

1952. *War and Peace.* Lithographic series on Balzac.

1954. Portraits of Sylvette. First appearance of Jacqueline. *Women of Algiers.*

1955-1956. The *Studio in Cannes* series.

1957. *Tauromachy* (aquatints). *The Maids of Honour.*

1958-1960. First series of linocuts.

1959. *The Village of Vauvenargues.*

1960-1961. *The Luncheons.*

1961-1962. Second series of linocuts.

1963. *The Painter and His Model.* Opening of the Picasso Museum in Barcelona.

1966. Great exhibition of homage to Picasso in Paris.

1967. Erotic and burlesque drawings.

1968. The *Suite Crommelinck*: 347 engravings.

1970. *Characters,* exhibited at the Palace of the Popes in Avignon.

1971. Several vividly coloured drawings.

1972. The second *Suite Crommelinck.* A new series of *Characters.*

1973. April 8: death of Picasso at Notre-Dame-de-Vie (Mougins). On April 10 he is buried at Vauvenargues. May 23: opening of a great exhibition of *Characters* shown for the first time, at the Palace of the Popes in Avignon.

J.P.F.

1. *Picasso with his sister Lola. Malaga, around 1888.*

2. ***Hercules with His Club.*** *Malaga, 1890. Even as a child Picasso endeavoured to make ''regular'' drawings, following a model...*

3. ***Picador.*** *Malaga, around 1890. One of the great themes of his life was first depicted by the artist when he was only eight or nine years old, possibly after his father had taken him to a bullfight.*

1

3

2

4

5

4. **The Sick Woman.** *Corunna, 1894.*
*In this little picture we seem to find a
forerunner of his picture* Science and
Charity.

5. **Beggar in a Cap.** *Corunna, 1895.*
*At the age of thirteen Picasso introduced
one of the themes which he was to develop
during the Blue Period: that of the
forsaken.*

6

7

6. **Country Scene.** *Corunna, 1895.*
   *The most surprising features of this little
   picture are the freshness of the
   brushstroke, the fact that things are hinted
   at with such acumen and, above all, the
   light tones.*

7. **Portrait of Dr Pérez Costales.**
   Corunna, 1895.
   *The self-assured aplomb of this character
   contrasts with the attitude of the Beggar
   and shows us the artist's psychological
   insight.*

8

8. **Old Fisherman.** *Malaga, summer 1895.*
We know that this old fisherman was called Salmerón, that he hired himself out as a model and that Picasso finished this picture so quickly that he quite disconcerted his relatives. The artist, though at this time only thirteen years old, is not content merely to record the sitter's features, but seems to be trying to penetrate his very soul.

9

10

9. ***Alicante from the Ship.*** *1895.*
   All Picasso's comings and goings between Malaga and Barcelona were by sea. From the deck he used to draw the places the ship passed or the ports she called at: Cartagena, Alicante, Valencia...

10. ***View of the Port of Valencia.*** *1895.*

11

11. ***Portrait of the Artist's Mother.*** *Barcelona, 1896.*
    This pastel reveals the artist's technical ability and his turn for portraiture at the age of fourteen...

12. ***She-ass.*** *Barcelona, 1896.*
    The spectacle afforded by the streets of Barcelona immediately attracted the lad from Andalusia, who wanted to capture every aspect of the city. Since he lived near the Born (the central market), his neighbourhood was always full of carts and horses...

13. ***Catalan Wearing Typical Peasant's Cap and other sketches.*** *Barcelona, 1895.*
    This man wearing the typical Phrygian cap of the Catalan peasantry was most probably a carter Picasso had seen at the main railway station (the "French" station) or at the Born market. This water-colour looks as fresh today as though it had just been finished... The notes we see around it are evidence of the artist's curiosity.

12

13

14

15

14. **Sketch for "Science and Charity".**
    Barcelona, 1897.

15. **Sketch for "Science and Charity".**
    Barcelona, 1897.

16. **Science and Charity.** *Barcelona, 1897.*
    *A comparison of the finished picture with the
    two preceding sketches will give us some idea of
    the way Picasso worked. The characters change
    their attitudes, their clothes and their
    expressions. Picasso wanted to capture life "on
    the wing", so to speak. His art was to be
    dynamic all his life. Sometimes, however, he had
    to paint great compositions to take part in
    competitions or collective exhibitions, as in this
    picture. But the artist's true genius is revealed
    in the two sketches much more than in the
    finished work.*

17. **"Salón del Prado".** *Madrid, 1897.*
    *There is no such thing as bad weather when
    you have spring in your heart. For a painter
    the rain is just another possibility of expressing
    himself, as is shown in this note Picasso did in
    Madrid.*

18. **Portrait of Philip IV** (after Velázquez).
    Madrid, 1897.
    *Never, perhaps, had Picasso shown such
    willingness to be obedient as during his stay in
    Madrid in 1897, as we can see from this copy
    of Velázquez's portrait of Philip IV.*

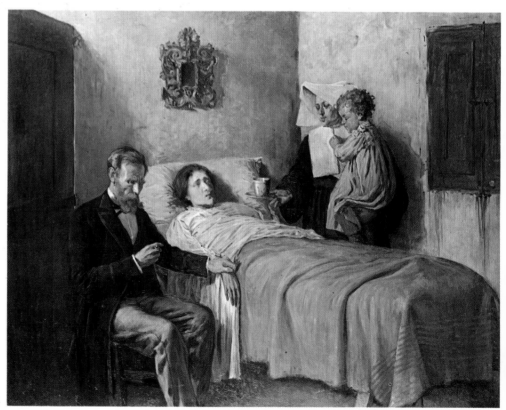

16

17

18

19

20

21

22

19. **Mule.** *Ports del Maestrat, 1898.*
    Picasso's affection for animals, which lasted all his life, seems to be reflected in the look of this mule... But no kind of sentimentalism softens the brushwork, which is lively in the extreme.

20. **"Mas del Quiquet".** *Ports del Maestrat, 1898.*
    On very few occasions was the artist to depict a landscape in such idyllic tones as those he used when staying at Horta de Sant Joan.

21. **Seated Woman Reading.**
    Barcelona, 1899-1900.
    Even when he seems to concentrate on detail, as in this case, the artist is always essentially sober.

22. **The Riera de Sant Joan, Seen from a Window.** *Barcelona, 1900.*
    The studio he shared with Casagemas in the Riera de Sant Joan is perhaps the most celebrated of all Picasso's studios in Barcelona.

23. **Portrait of Lola.** *Barcelona, 1899.*
    Any old piece of paper was good enough for this young artist to use for a little masterpiece, like this portrait of his sister. In the signature we can see a hint of his growing dynamism.

23

24. **Sketch for the menu of the "4 Gats".** *Barcelona, 1900. Pere Romeu, the manager of the 4 Gats, used this work as the menu for his establishment.*

25. **Manola** *(inspired by Lola Ruiz Picasso). Barcelona, 1900. Sometimes a face, a person, can be a pretext for a composition, a harmony of colours.*

26. **Sabartés as a "Decadent Poet".** *Barcelona, 1900. It was most probably Sabartés himself who gave his portrait its title, of a sort much in fashion at the time. In this portrait of his friend the artist, besides his concern for a likeness, seems to have attempted to sum up the spirit of Modernisme (the Catalan version of Art Nouveau).*

24

25

26

27. **Portrait of Sebastià Junyer-Vidal.** *Barcelona, 1900.*
The fashion for all things Wagnerian in Barcelona was so widespread that it reached into every sphere of life. Here we have Sebastià Junyer-Vidal with his name germanicized and a rather Kaiser-like moustache.

28. **Bullfighters and Bull Waiting for the Next Move.** *Barcelona, 1900.*
Being an Andalusian, Picasso was a keen bullfighting aficionado *all his life and succeeded in capturing every aspect of the spectacle, as in this extraordinarily vivid little study, in pastel and tempera, which now hangs in the Cau Ferrat Museum in Sitges.*

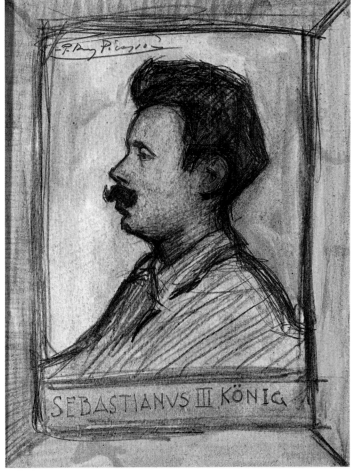

27

28

29

30

31

32

33

29. **In the Dressing-room.**
    Paris, 1900.
    *This study is Parisian in feeling,
    not just on account of the subject
    but because the technique used
    with the pastel inevitably reminds
    us of Degas.*

30. **Nursemaid with Two Children.**
    Paris, 1900.
    *In his tiny sketch-book the artist
    drew everything he saw in the
    street, with a power of synthesis
    reminiscent of that of certain
    Chinese artists.*

31. **Seated Woman, Full-face.**
    Paris, 1900.
    *In Picasso's "Paris, 1900" sketch-
    book, as at all times in the
    artist's career, women occupy a
    most preponderant place.*

32. **The Embrace in the Street.**
    Paris, 1900.
    *Picasso, always observant, was
    attracted by anything representing
    a novelty to him. And one of
    these novelties, in the Paris of
    1900, was the sight of couples
    embracing in the street.*

33. **Two Female Figures.**
    Paris, 1900.
    *Another of the novelties of Paris
    for Picasso was the sight of
    women sitting in cafés and
    drinking. Here the artist gives us
    reliable evidence on the point.*

34

35

36

37

34. **Silhouettes from Toledo.**
Toledo or Madrid, 1901.
From Madrid Picasso made the journey to
Toledo and back in one day. This was
sufficient for him to capture some scenes
and certain characters with great
accuracy.

35. **Bullfighting Scene.** Barcelona, 1901.
This work seems to have been done in
Barcelona but signed in Paris, in which
latter place it was doubtless exhibited.

36. **Female Nude.** Paris, 1901.
This is one of the very few pictures the
artist ever painted with his model in front
of him.

37. **The Red Skirt.** Paris, 1901.
If Picasso's Parisian pastels remind one of
Degas, those he did the following year
have a violence of colour that tends more
to the expressionistic.

38

38. **Woman in a Bonnet.** *Paris, 1901.*
   Both in its subject — an inmate of the women's prison — and in its blue-green colouring, this work may be regarded as one of the first in the Blue Period.

39

39. **Large Blue Self-portrait.** *Paris, 1901.*
*If we could compare the euphoric self-portraits painted when he had just arrived in
Paris with this one done at the end of the same year, we should understand
Picasso's whole evolution. His face here looks as though he were almost starving.*

40

41

42

40. **_Picasso at the "4 Gats"._** _Barcelona, 1902._
    On his return to Barcelona, Picasso resumed his regular visits to the 4 Gats. Here
    we see him at a table with (from left to right) Pere Romeu, Josep Rocarol, Emili
    Fontbona, Àngel F. de Soto and Jaume Sabartés (standing).

41. **_Woman in a Shawl._** _Barcelona, 1902._
    We are now at the height of the Blue Period, and with one of its leitmotivs, _a_
    woman.

42. **_Woman Huddled on the Ground in Pensive Mood._** _Barcelona, 1902._
    What was it that led Picasso, in 1902, to identify so deeply with the solitude and
    sadness of women?

43

44

43. **Roofs of Barcelona.** *Barcelona, 1903.*
*From his studio in the Riera de Sant Joan
the artist painted the roofs in front of his
window. In his work we are always equally
likely to find the products of his sense of
fantasy or sober, severe notes like this one.*

44. **Couple with a Child in a Café.**
Barcelona, 1903.
*The chronicles of the Barcelona of his day
that Picasso gives us in painting and
drawing are by no means flattering to the
city.*

45. **Mother and Child on the Seashore.**
Barcelona, 1902.
*Amid the desolation of the waters this
silhouette of a woman, somewhat Gothic in
structure, holds a red flower as a symbol of
hope...*

45

46

47

46. **Self-portrait Looking over His Shoulder.** *Paris, 1902-1903.*
*The way in which the artist is looking behind him in this self-portrait is very
evident. It is not an exclusively aesthetic pose or one adopted for portraiture.
Picasso here is taking leave of his immediate past.*

47. **Simian Self-portrait.** *Paris, 1st January 1903.*
*The ability to see oneself objectively and a sense of humour are both signs of
mental health and show that one has not lost one's self-control.*

48

48. **Portrait of Corina Romeu.** *Barcelona, 1902.*
*This portrait of the wife of Pere Romeu, manager of the 4 Gats, was originally
oval and hung for a long time in their establishment.*

49

49. ***Poor People on the Seashore*** (The Tragedy). *Barcelona, 1903.*
Few of the scenes we find in the great theatre of the Blue Period are as moving as
this one. Equally few those in which the light — the purples and mauves — is as
successfully resolved.

50. **Life.** *Barcelona, 1903.*
Inspired by the suicide of Picasso's friend Casagemas, this picture may be considered a synthesis, as regards story and pictorial technique, of the central motifs of the Blue Period. It tells us several things simultaneously.

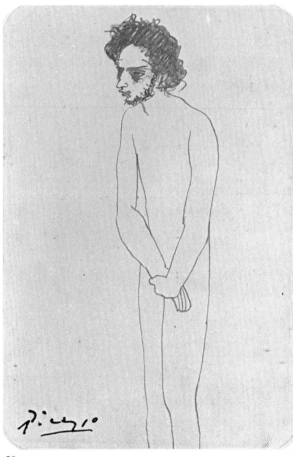

51

52

51. **The Blue Glass.** *Barcelona, 1903.*
This picture might just as well be called The Red Flower, *but the reference to blue links it more immediately to the Blue Period.*

52. **Casagemas Naked.** *Barcelona, 1904.*
In a few strokes this drawing evokes the whole drama of Casagemas.
The deep shadows encircling his eyes and the ashamed attitude form an expressive synthesis. Perhaps everything Picasso was trying to tell us in Life *is said here in an abridged form.*

53. **The Madman.** *Barcelona, 1904.*
Everything is poor in this water-colour, in which there seems to be more water than colour; the work is drawn on pieces of wrapping paper stuck together and the madman's epileptic gesture seems to be trying to infect us, even today, with his despair.

53

54. **The Frugal Repast.** *Paris, 1904.*
*Picasso had done only one etching before this one, that of the "left-handed"
picador, which he did in Barcelona in 1899. But it was now that his career as an
engraver really began, after the technical advice given by the painter Ricard
Canals.*

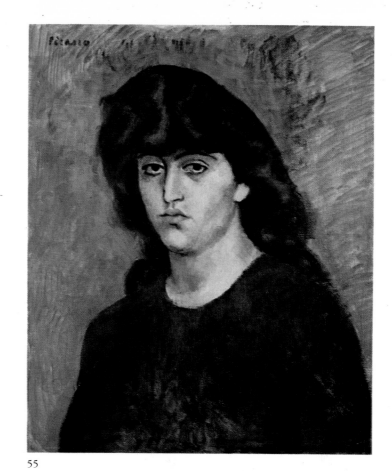

55. **Portrait of Suzanne Bloch.**
Paris, 1904.
In Paris the Blue Period was gradually transformed, losing much of its dramatic character...

56. **Woman Leaning Forward.**
Paris, 1904.
While the attitude of this woman reminds us of those painted in Barcelona, the brushwork reveals a new preponderance of plastic values, which in this case almost reach the point of abstraction.

55

56

57

57. ***The Woman with the Raven.*** *Paris, 1904.*
    The slightly metallic ultramarine blue of the background contrasts with the
    expressionism of the composition and underlines it.

58

58. **Woman Sleeping** (Meditation). *Paris, autumn 1904.*
Between the Blue Period and the Rose Period there are a few compositions, like this one, in which the autumn ochres predominate.

59

59. *Family of Acrobats with an Ape.* Paris, 1905.
Theatre life seen from behind the scenes interested Picasso much more than the
performances themselves.

60

61

60. **Group of Acrobats.** *Paris, 1905.*
In this little water-colour we find
a synthesis of many of the themes
of the Rose Period.

61. **Seated Ape.** *Paris, 1905.*
The sobriety and precision of the
line could hardly be greater, as
though the artist had been
observing this monkey all his life.

62

63

62. **Boy with a Dog.** *Paris, 1905.*
This work is considered to belong to the Rose Period, but the preponderance of blue shows that the boundary between the two periods is difficult to establish exactly.

63. **Double sketch for "Acrobat on a Ball".** *Paris, 1905.*
Before undertaking a major work Picasso always explored its possibilities...

64. **Acrobat on a Ball.** *Paris, 1905.*
The fresco-like qualities to be detected in the background of this composition seem to foretell certain problems that would arise with the advent of Cubism.

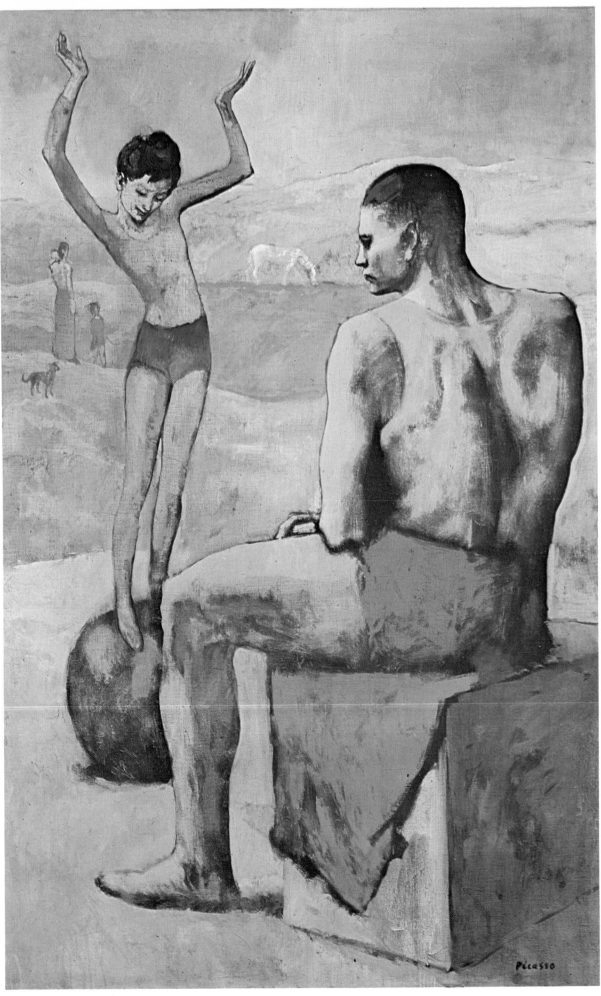

64

65. **Hurdy-gurdy Man, Standing.**
Paris, 1905.
A sketch that gives us the whole character.

66. **Equestrienne on Horseback.**
Paris, 1905.
The whole poetry of the circus seems to be condensed in this painting, in tempera on cardboard.

67. **Family of Acrobats.** *Paris, 1905.*
The loneliness of the place brings out the loneliness of the characters; the races taking place in the background seem to form part of another world.

68. **A Boat on the Canal.**
Schoorldam, 1905.
In his sketch-books Picasso left us convincing evidence of his stay in Holland.

66

67

68

69

69. ***Boy with a Pipe.*** *Paris, 1905.*
   *The character here is still "Blue", but the background is "Rose". The wreath of
   flowers crowning the boy's head seems to be an attempt to give visual charm
   priority over any dramatic quality.*

70

70. **Woman with a Fan.** *Paris, 1905.*
The influence of Egyptian art and a farewell to the Blue Period within the Rose Period.

71

72

71. **Boy and Horse.** *Paris, 1906.*
*Here the artist seems to have taken
pleasure in recording the beauty of
the animal as much as that of the
boy leading it.*

72. **Sketch for ''Arcady''.**
Paris, 1906.
*A breath of fresh air now invades
the painter's works. It is the voice of
nature calling him.*

73. **La Toilette.**
Gósol, spring-summer 1906.
*The idea of Mediterranean beauty
and of a ''Greek'' Catalonia is the
inspiration for this celebrated
composition, painted in a little
village in the Catalan Pyrenees.*

73

74

74. **Fernande on a Mule.**
    Gósol, spring-summer 1906.
    With the mass of the Pedraforca in the background...

75. **Still Life with Drinking-Vessel.**
    Gósol, spring-summer 1906.
    The traditional two-spouted drinking-vessel known as a porró *was always regarded by Picasso as one of the "identifying marks" of Catalonia.*

76. **The Woman with the Loaves.**
    Gósol, spring-summer 1906.
    A figure that has become famous through postcard versions. The ochres here have very evidently ousted the rose tones.

77

78

77. **Fernande with a Kerchief on Her Head.** *Gósol, spring-summer 1906. Fernande's figure is stylized here like that of the village women painted at Gósol, but this stylization is possibly due to a fresh influence from El Greco, on whom Miquel Utrillo had just published a monograph.*

78. **Young Gósol Man Wearing Catalan Cap.** *Gósol, summer 1906. All the figures wearing the typical Phrygian cap which we know to have been painted at Gósol are shown wearing it with the pointed end handing down behind.*

79. **Large Standing Nude.** *Gósol, spring-summer 1906. Greece? Classicism? Mediterraneanism? Perhaps much less than any of them, and yet much more: the beauty of woman, naked and without attributes.*

79

80

80. **_Portrait of Gertrude Stein._** _Paris, 1906._
_This portrait became a positive battlefield for Picasso. The conversion of the face
into a mask is one of the most visible struggles._

81

81. **Self-portrait with a Palette in His Hand.** *Paris, summer-autumn 1906.*
The artist's wondering eyes seem to convey a sense of expectation regarding what is happening to him...

82

82. **Study for "Two Women Arm in Arm".** *Paris, summer-autumn 1906.*
From the pictoral point of view, these two women are half-way between those painted at Gósol and the ones preceding Cubism.

83. **Head in Half-profile from the Left.** *Paris, autumn 1906.*
The search for simplified structures of the human face.

84. **Two Female Nudes.** *Paris, autumn-winter 1906.*
Neither female beauty nor anything else can distract Picasso from his exclusively plastic research.

83

84 Picasso

85

86

85. ***Bust of a Woman with Her Eyes Closed.*** *Paris, spring 1907.*
The search for simplified structures is parallel to the artist's research in colouring.

86. ***Bust of a Woman in Half-profile from the Left.***
Paris, spring-summer 1907.
The colour at times becomes strident and almost elementary.

87. ***One of the "Demoiselles".*** *Paris, spring-summer 1907.*
The structures finally seem to be at one with the colours...

88. ***Bust of a "Demoiselle".*** *Paris, summer 1907.*
The results obtained by the artist in some of his discoveries bring his work close to the art of primitive peoples.

87

88

89. **Les Demoiselles d'Avignon.**
Paris, summer 1907.
This work represented a great upheaval in the
art of the West and the starting-point for a new
art.

89

90

90. **Landscape with Two Figures.** *Paris (?), summer 1908.*
The figures here are so closely integrated with the landscape that they almost blend into it. We have to look for them.

91

91. **Bather.** *Paris, winter 1908-1909.*
The very word Cubism may be misleading, as in this case, with regard to the true
content of this artistic movement.

92

92. ***Bread and Fruit-Dish on a Table.*** *Paris, early 1909.*

93. ***Portrait of Fernande.*** *Horta de Sant Joan, summer 1909.*
The influence of Cézanne is still visible, but the geometrizing tendency is increasing...

94

94. ***The Pond in Horta.*** *Horta de Sant Joan, summer 1909.*
*The most characteristic part of the work Picasso painted at Horta may be described
as geometric Cubism.*

95

95. **_Girl with a Mandoline._** _Paris, early 1910._
    The two halves of this work express the struggle then taking place: in the lower half
    we see the three dimensions, while the upper part is totally flat.

96

96. ***The Guitarist.*** *Cadaqués, summer 1910.*
*The achievement of flat painting coincided in Picasso's work with the achievement
of abstraction.*

97

97. _Portrait of Daniel-Henry Kahnweiler._ _Paris, autumn 1910._
The artist seems here to have solved the problem of portraiture with that of
bidimensionality.

98

98. ***Landscape near Ceret.*** *Ceret, summer 1911.*
Abstraction continues, but we are beginning to glimpse some elements of reality.

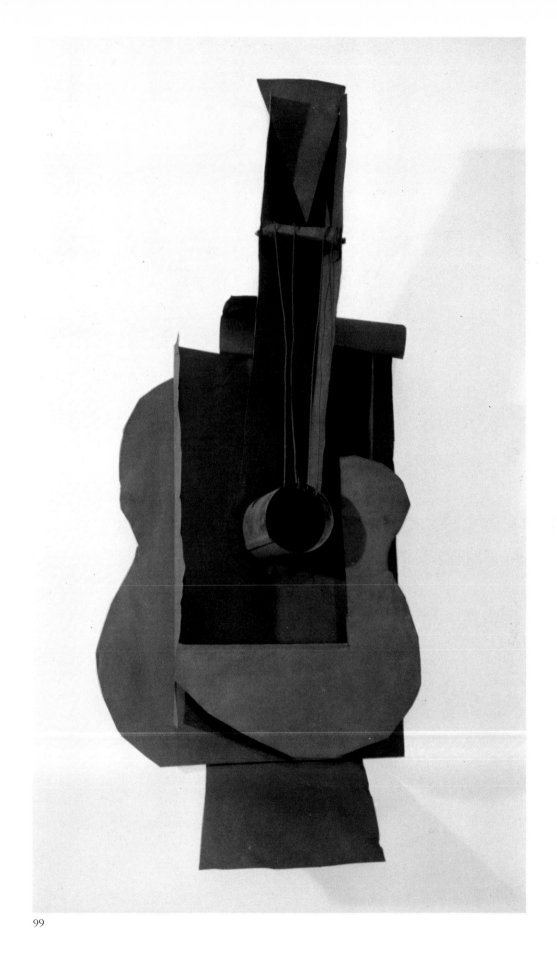

99

99. **Guitar.** *Paris, early 1912.*
   Cubism was by now a fully mature language, capable of expressing everything and with all sorts of different materials.

100. ***The Violin*** *(Jolie Eva). Ceret, spring 1912.*
"Pretty Eva", "I love Eva"... The fact is, however, that Eva was the only one of Picasso's mistresses that he never painted.

101. ***Still Life with Chair Caning.*** *Paris, May 1912.*
This work is supposed to be the first in which Picasso used papier collé, *in this case to represent the wicker seat of the chair.*

102. ***The Scallop Shell.*** *(Notre Avenir est dans l'air). Paris, spring 1912.*
Picasso resorts to the oval structure at a time when it seems to have fallen into total disuse.

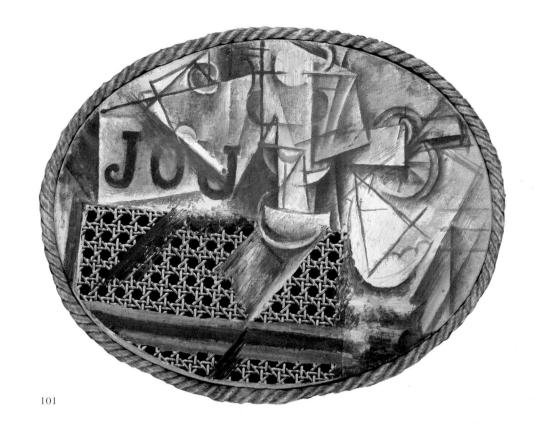

101

102

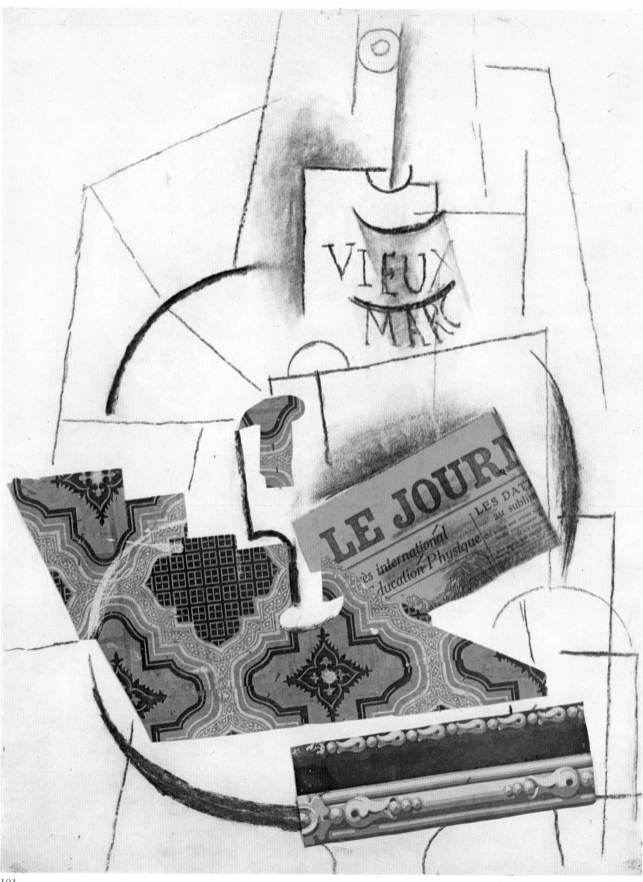

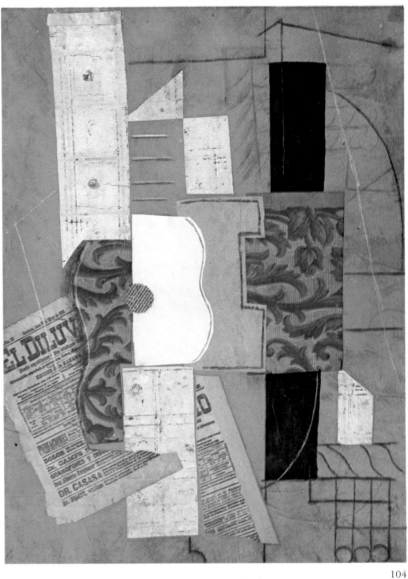

104

103. **_Bottle of Vieux Marc, Glass
and Newspaper._** _Ceret, spring 1913.
This is one of the best-known and
most typical of the_ papiers collés.

104. **_Guitar._** _Ceret, spring 1913.
The_ papiers collés _are a "tangible"
element that counterbalance the
earlier abstraction._

105. **_Head._** _Paris or Ceret, early 1913.
The pyramidal structure also
persists in the_ papiers collés.

105

106

106. _Woman in an Armchair._ _Paris, autumn 1913._
Here Cubism combines with figurative art once again.

107

107. ***Portrait of a Young Girl.*** *Avignon, summer 1914.*
   All the elements in this work are painted, though some of them may seem to have been stuck on.

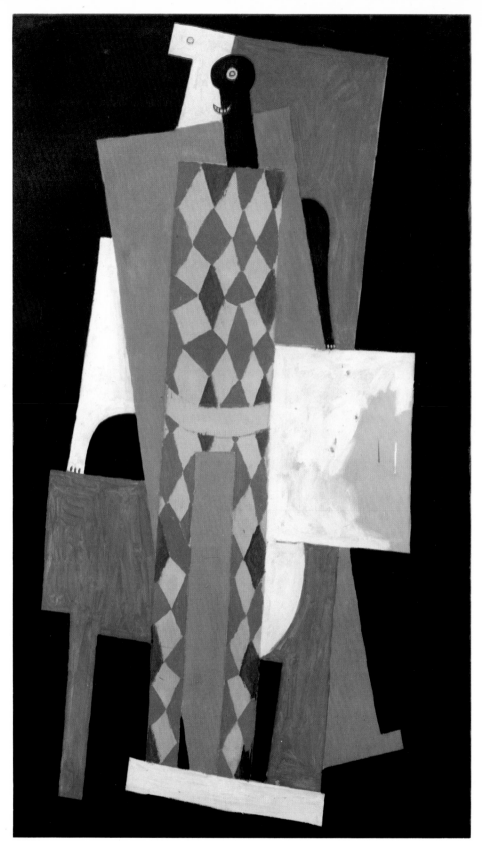

108

108. **Harlequin.** *Paris, late 1915.*
The will to make a flat painting is satisfied here without having to renounce reality altogether.

109. **Manola with Pointilliste Technique.** *Barcelona, 1917.*
Pointillisme *was one of the forms taken by post-Impressionism. But Picasso's version of* pointillisme *was a very personal one.*

110. **The Barcelona Harlequin.**
Barcelona, 1917.
This harlequin certainly deserves its title, for it was painted in Barcelona and was given by Picasso to the museum of that city in 1919.

111. **Bathers.**
Biarritz, summer 1918.
What can be the origin of such stylization in the creator of Cubism? Can we, perhaps, speak in this case of Pompeian colours?

112. **Sleeping Peasants.**
Paris, 1919.
If we did not know that this work was by Picasso, it would be very difficult to guess it. Here Picasso is "another", as he was to be on many other occasions.

113

113. **Seated Woman.** *Paris, 1920.*
   The fleshy forms, already apparent in the hands of the Barcelona Harlequin, *are now absolutely in the ascendant.*

114

115

114. **Three Musicians.**
Fontainebleau, summer 1921.
Here the Italian influence is certainly visible.
The liveliness of the colours in this new
Cubism contrasts with the austerity of many of
the stages in the first Cubist period.

115. **Portrait of Igor Stravinsky.**
Paris, 24 May, 1920.
Picasso did a few portraits using line only;
but it was line of devastating precision.

116

116. ***Three Women at the Spring.*** *Fontainebleau, summer 1921.*
Around the same time as he painted Three Musicians *(flat painting), Picasso did this work, composed entirely of volume and relief.*

117

117. **_Harlequin._** *Paris, 1923.*
    It is not generally known that the model for the three most famous of the 1923 harlequins was the Catalan painter Jacint Salvadó. Here we have the one which, in homage to the painter, was hung in the Louvre for several weeks in the place usually occupied by the Gioconda.

118

118. **Paulo as Harlequin.** *Paris, 1924.*
This is the painter's little son, whom the French called Paulo to distinguish him from his father.

119. **Wineglass and Packet of Cigarettes.** *Paris, 1924.*
Cubism assumed the most widely-varying forms before disappearing...

120. **Studio with Plaster Head.** *Juan-les-Pins (Provence), summer 1925.*
Picasso's visits to the Mediterranean always increased the pleasure he took in colour...

119

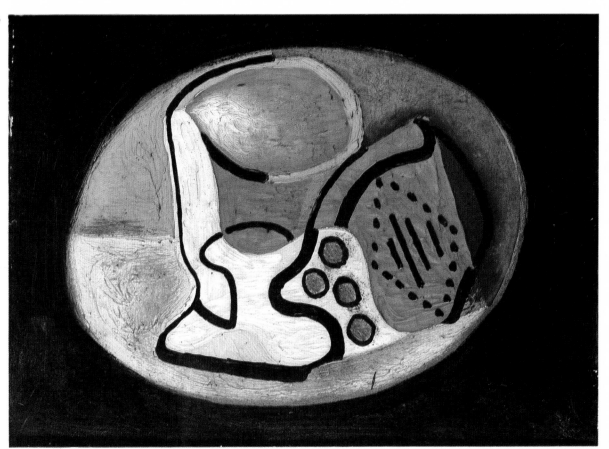

120

121

121. **The Dance.** *Paris, 1925.*
After a period of works in a rather pleasant vein, this one surprises us with its syncopated, almost ferocious accents...

122

123

122. **Wire Construction** *(model for the monument to Guillaume Apollinaire).*
Paris, 1928.
Apollinaire had always represented the avant-garde, and the monument his friend conceived for him was as advanced as he could make it.

123. **The Studio.** *Paris, 1927-1928.*
Flat Cubism, but also a coded language through a possible bust and a possible figure with three eyes.

124

124. **Girl before a Mirror.** *Boisgeloup, March 1932.*
There may be some influence of stained-glass techniques here, but the
predominance of curves leads me to include this work in the "curvist" period.

125

125. **Bather with Beach Ball.** Boisgeloup, August 1932.
Picasso here transposes his capacity for mimetism to the object represented. Thus the bather seems to be absolutely infected by the spherical form of the ball she is playing with.

126

126. **_Guernica._** _Paris, 1937._
    A synthesis of all the artist's previous periods, with Cubism and Expressionism
    predominant, but with an epic spirit that is entirely new.

127

127. *Head of a Woman Weeping.* *Paris, 24 May 1937.*
Done at the same time as Guernica, *this head already contains some of the dislocated elements that were soon to predominate in Picasso's work.*

128

128. **Weeping Woman.** *Paris, October 1937.*
In this head, which was painted some months after Guernica, *and in which the eyes have been transformed into little boats on the point of being wrecked, there is an explosion of all the colours that the sobriety of* Guernica *had concealed from us.*

129

129. **Women at Their Toilette** *(Cartoon for a tapestry). Paris, spring 1938.*
The lively colours here, plus the equal liveliness of the *papiers collés (eliminated in* Guernica), *seem to rebuild a happy world...*

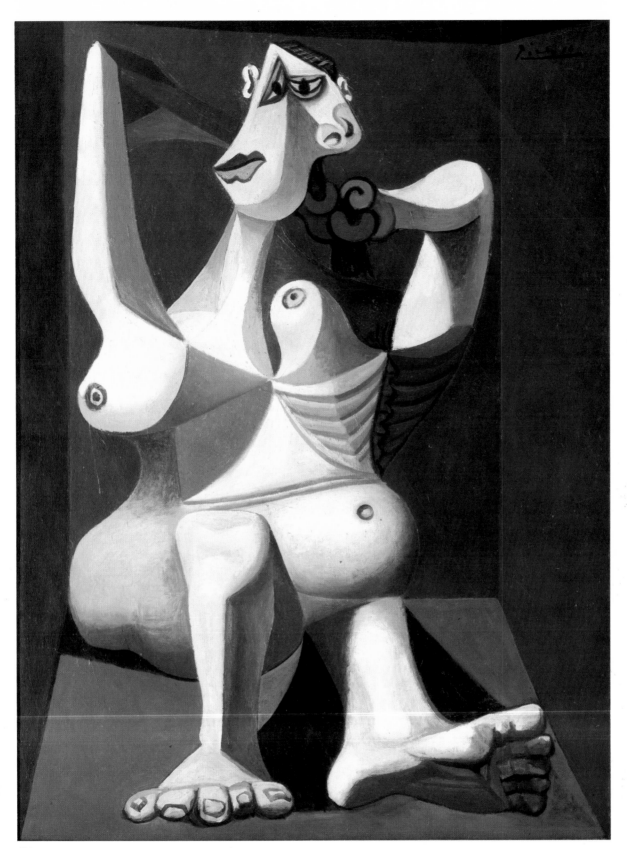

130

130. **Woman Dressing Her Hair.** *Royan, June 1940.*
*The second World War has begun and the vision of the world offered here by the
artist seems conditioned by that horrifying looking-glass.*

131. **Stylized Woman's Head on a Black Background.** *November 1945.
Here the artist succeeds in travelling back through time and bringing forth his ancestral origin, his primitive vision of things.*

132. **Bull.** *December 1945.
Picasso's exploration of the past brings the "rediscovery" of the bull, a feature of all Mediterranean cultures.*

133

133. **Man with Sheep.** *Paris, 1944.*
The "primitivism" of the sculpture brings us to the primitive nature of the scene...

134

134. **Bull.** *Vallauris, 1947.*
Real and phantasmagorical, fearful and familiar, close and remote, the
"measure" of the bull here assumes the "measurelessness" of dreams.

135

136

135 to 137. **Plates.** *Vallauris, 1947-1948. Picasso's powers of variation are here exercised on ceramics and seem to be truly inexhaustible.*

137

138

138. **The Studio in Cannes.** *Cannes, March 1956.*
Who lives in this room? The unpainted canvas we see in the centre is a possibility opening on to the future...

139. **The Maids of Honour** *(Ensemble). Cannes, 4 September 1957.*
Can all the characters in Velázquez's great work be fitted into a little composition? How can one resolve a work like that in the language of contemporary painting?

140. **The Maids of Honour.** *(Infanta Margarita María). Cannes, 28 August 1957.*
The charm of the Infanta may well be expressed through the charm of the brushstroke...

141. **The Maids of Honour** *(Ensemble, without Velázquez or Mari-Bárbola).*
Cannes, 17 November 1957.
Can rhythm alone solve the problem of Velázquez's representation?

139

140

141

142

143

142. ***The Maids of Honour***
(The doves, 1).
Cannes, 6 September 1957.
The outside world here affords us some relief from the excessive problems we face in interpreting Velázquez's work.

143. ***The Maids of Honour.***
(The doves, 5).
Cannes, 7 September 1957.
The mineral world (earth-sea), the plant world (groves) and the animal world (doves) often possess therapeutic faculties.

144. ***The Maids of Honour*** *(Isabel de Velasco).*
Cannes, 30 December 1957.
Just before the end of the year the Maids of Honour, through the childlike gesture of reconciliation of one of their number, take their leave.

144

145. **Bust of Woman Wearing a Hat.** *1962.*
   The sculptor's knife and chisel can carve a decided and decisive furrow in order
   to obtain from a sheet of linoleum all its possibilities of expression.

146. **Luncheon on the Grass (Le déjeuner sur l'herbe), after Manet.**
   Vauvenargues, March-August 1960.
   Manet? Picasso? Where do the characters begin and nature finish?

147. **Aquatint.** *Mougins, 25 May 1968.*
   This is one of the 347 engravings done by Picasso between 16 March and
   5 October 1968, in which the technique joins the mystery of composition.

146

147

148

148. **Man's Head.** *Mougins, 9 July 1971.*
One of the last portrayals of a Catalan in the typical
peasant's cap...

149. **Character.** *Mougins, 19 January 1972.*
The brush seems to be trying to be quicker than thought, as quick
as the eye itself.

150. **Man's Head.** *Mougins, 30 April 1972.*
The characters are becoming extravagant or grotesque.

149

150

INDEX OF ILLUSTRATIONS

1. Picasso with his sister Lola.
Malaga, around 1888.

2. **Hercules with His Club.**
Malaga, November 1890.
Lead pencil on paper, 49.5 × 32 cm.
Picasso Museum, Barcelona.

3. **Picador.**
Malaga, around 1890.
Oil on wood, 24 × 19 cm.
Heirs of the artist.

4. **The Sick Woman.**
Corunna, 1894.
Oil on wood.
Dimensions unknown.
Heirs of the artist.

5. **Beggar in a Cap.**
Corunna, 1895.
Oil on canvas, 65 × 50 cm.
Heirs of the artist.

6. **Country Scene.**
Corunna, 1895.
Oil on paper, 12.8 × 19 cm.
Picasso Museum, Barcelona.

7. **Portrait of Dr Pérez Costales.**
Corunna, 1895.
Oil on canvas, 52 × 37 cm.
Heirs of the artist.

8. **Old Fisherman.**
Malaga, summer 1895.
Oil on canvas, 82 × 62 cm.
Sala Collection, Montserrat Abbey
(Barcelona).

9. **Alicante from the Ship.**
September 1895.
Oil on wood, 9.9 × 15.5 cm.
Picasso Museum, Barcelona.

10. **View of the Port of Valencia.**
From the ship, September 1895.
Oil on wood, 10.1 × 15.5 cm.
Picasso Museum, Barcelona.

11. **Portrait of the Artist's Mother.**
Barcelona, 1896.
Pastel on paper, 49.8 × 39 cm.
Picasso Museum, Barcelona.

12. **She-ass.**
Barcelona, 1896.
Oil on wood, 9.8 × 15.5 cm.
Picasso Museum, Barcelona.

13. **Catalan Wearing Typical
Peasant's Cap and other sketches.**
Barcelona, 1895.
Water-colour on paper.
Upper part of a double drawing
measuring, 48 × 21.3 cm.
Picasso Museum, Barcelona.

14. **Sketch for "Science and Charity".**
Barcelona, 1897.
Water-colour on paper, 22.8 × 28.6 cm.
Picasso Museum, Barcelona.

15. **Sketch for "Science and Charity".**
Barcelona, 1897.
Oil on wood, 19.6 × 27.3 cm.
Picasso Museum, Barcelona.

16. **Science and Charity.**
Barcelona, 1897.
Oil on canvas, 197 × 249.4 cm.
Picasso Museum, Barcelona.

17. **"Salón del Prado".**
Madrid, 1897.
Oil on wood, 10 × 15.5 cm.
Picasso Museum, Barcelona.

18. **Portrait of Philip IV** (after Velázquez).
Madrid, 1897.
Oil on canvas, 54.2 × 46.7 cm.
Picasso Museum, Barcelona.

19. **Mule.**
Ports del Maestrat, summer 1898.
Oil on canvas, 27.7 × 36.4 cm.
Picasso Museum, Barcelona.

20. **"Mas del Quiquet".**
Ports del Maestrat, summer 1898.
Oil on canvas, 27 × 40 cm.
Picasso Museum, Barcelona.

21. **Seated Woman Reading.**
Barcelona, 1899-1900.
Water-colour on paper, 19.1 × 13.9 cm.
Picasso Museum, Barcelona.

22. **The Riera de Sant Joan, Seen from
a Window.**
Barcelona, 1900.
Oil on wood, 22.1 × 13.8 cm.
Picasso Museum, Barcelona.

23. **Portrait of Lola.**
Barcelona, 1899.
Sepia on paper, 23.1 × 17 cm.
Heirs of the artist.

24. **Sketch for the menu of the "4 Gats".**
Barcelona, 1900.
Pen-and-ink and colour, 22 × 16 cm.
Present whereabouts unknown.

25. **Manola** (inspired by Lola Ruiz
Picasso).
Barcelona, 1900.
Pastel, 44.5 × 21 cm.
Miss Barbara Thurston Collection,
New York.

26. **Sabartés as a "Decadent Poet".**
Barcelona, 1900.
Charcoal and water-colour on paper,
48 × 32 cm.
Picasso Museum, Barcelona.

27. **Portrait of Sebastià Junyer-Vidal.**
Barcelona, 1900.
Lead pencil, coloured pencil and
water-colour, varnished, 21 × 16 cm.
Picasso Museum, Barcelona.

28. **Bullfighters and Bull Waiting
for the Next Move.**
Barcelona, 1900.
Pastel and gouache, 16.2 × 30.5 cm.
Cau Ferrat Museum, Sitges (Barcelona).

29. **In the Dressing-room.**
Paris, 1900.
Pastel on paper, 48 × 53 cm.
Picasso Museum, Barcelona.

30. **Nursemaid with Two Children.**
Paris, 1900.
Lead pencil and water-colour on paper,
10.5 × 6 cm.
Picasso Museum, Barcelona.

31. **Seated Woman, Full-face.**
Paris, 1900.
Lead pencil, water-colour and pastel on
paper, 10.5 × 6 cm.
Picasso Museum, Barcelona.

32. **The Embrace in the Street.**
Paris, 1900.
Pastel on paper, 59 × 35 cm.
Picasso Museum, Barcelona.

33. **Two Female Figures.**
Paris, 1900.
Water-colour and ink on paper,
13.4 × 20.3 cm.
Cau Ferrat Museum, Sitges (Barcelona).

34. **Silhouettes from Toledo.**
Toledo or Madrid, 1901.
Charcoal and blue pencil, 16 × 24 cm.
Heirs of the artist.

35. **Bullfighting Scene** (The Victims).
Barcelona, spring 1901.
Oil on cardboard mounted on wood,
49.5 × 64.7 cm.
Stavros S. Niarchos Collection,
Saint-Moritz.

36. **Female Nude.**
Paris, spring-summer 1901.
Oil on canvas, 70 × 90.2 cm.
Musée National d'Art Moderne, Paris.

37. **The Red Skirt.**
Paris, 1901.
Pastel on paper, 55 × 47 cm.
Private collection, Tokyo.

38. **Woman in a Bonnet.**
Paris, 1901.
Oil on canvas, 41.3 × 33 cm.
Heirs of the artist.

39. **Large Blue Self-portrait.**
Paris, end of 1901.
Oil on canvas, 80 × 60 cm.
Musée Picasso, Paris.

40. **Picasso at the "4 Gats".**
Barcelona, 1902.
Pen-and-ink on paper, 31 × 34 cm.
Private collection, Canada.

41. **Woman in a Shawl.**
Barcelona, 1902.
Oil on canvas, 63 × 52.4 cm.
Heirs of the artist.

42. **Woman Huddled on the Ground in
Pensive Mood.**
Barcelona, 1902.
Oil on canvas, 63.5 × 50 cm.
C. B. Nathhorst Collection, Stockholm.

43. **Roofs of Barcelona.**
Barcelona, 1903.
Oil on canvas, 71 × 112 cm.
Heirs of the artist.

44. **Couple with a Child in a Café.**
Barcelona, 1903.
Pen-and-ink on paper, 21.9 × 16 cm.
Private collection, Barcelona.

45. **Mother and Child on the Seashore.**
Barcelona, 1902.
Oil on canvas, 83 × 60 cm.
Beyeler Collection, Basel.

46. **Self-portrait Looking over
His Shoulder.**
Paris, 1902-1903.
India ink on paper, 14 × 11 cm.
Mme. Jacqueline Apollinaire Collection,
Paris.

47. **Simian Self-portrait.**
Paris, 1st January 1903.
Pen-and-ink on paper, 11.8 × 10.7 cm.
Picasso Museum, Barcelona.

48. **Portrait of Corina Romeu.**
Barcelona, 1902.
Oil on canvas, 61 × 50 cm.
Heirs of the artist.

49. **Poor People on the Seashore**
(The Tragedy).
Barcelona, 1903.
Oil on wood, 105.4 × 69 cm.
The National Gallery of Art,
Washington, D.C.
Chester Dale Collection.

50. **Life.**
Barcelona, May 1903.
Oil on canvas, 197 × 127.3 cm.
The Cleveland Museum of Art,
Donation of the Hanna Foundation, 1945.

51. **The Blue Glass.**
Barcelona, 1903.
Oil on canvas, 66.1 × 28.5 cm.
Picasso Museum, Barcelona.

52. **Casagemas Naked.**
Barcelona, 1904.
Pen-and-ink and blue pencil, 13.3 × 9 cm.
Private collection, Barcelona.

53. **The Madman.**
Barcelona, 1904.
Blue water-colour on wrapping paper,
86 × 36 cm.
Picasso Museum, Barcelona.

54. **The Frugal Repast.**
Paris, September 1904.
Etching on a zinc plate, 50.9 × 41 cm.
Edition by Picasso, 1904, of fifteen or
twenty copies. There is a second edition by
Vollard of 250 copies.

55. **Portrait of Suzanne Bloch.**
Paris, 1904.
Oil on canvas, 65 × 54 cm.
Museu de Arte, São Paulo.

56. **Woman Leaning Forward.**
Paris, 1904.
Water-colour on paper, 27 × 36.8 cm.
The Museum of Modern Art, New York.

57. **The Woman with the Raven**
(first version).
Paris, 1904.
Gouache and pastel, 60.5 × 45.5 cm.
Private collection, Paris.

58. **Woman Sleeping** (Meditation).
Paris, autumn 1904.
Pen-and-ink and water-colour, 36.8 × 27 cm.
Mrs. Bertram Smith Collection, New York.

59. **Family of Acrobats with an Ape.**
Paris, 1905.
India ink, gouache, water-colour and pastel
on cardboard, 104 × 75 cm.
Göteborgs Kunstmuseum, Göteborg.

60. **Group of Acrobats.**
Paris, 1905.
India ink and water-colour on paper,
24 × 30.5 cm.
The Baltimore Museum of Art,
Cone Collection.

61. **Seated Ape.**
Paris, 1905.
Pen-and-ink and water-colour,
49.5 × 31.6 cm.
The Baltimore Museum of Art,
Cone Collection.

62. **Boy with a Dog.**
Paris, 1905.
Gouache, 57 × 41 cm.
Hermitage Museum, Leningrad.

63. **Double sketch for "Acrobat
on a Ball".**
Paris, 1905.
Gouache.
Dimensions unknown.
Hermitage Museum, Leningrad.

64. **Acrobat on a Ball.**
Paris, 1905.
Oil on canvas, 147 × 95 cm.
Pushkin Museum, Moscow.

65. **Hurdy-gurdy Man, Standing.**
Paris, 1905.
India ink on paper, 16 × 12 cm.
Heirs of the artist.

66. **Equestrienne on Horseback.**
Paris, 1905.
Gouache on cardboard, 60 × 79 cm.
Heirs of the artist.

67. **Family of Acrobats.**
Paris, 1905.
Gouache on cardboard, 51.2 × 61.2 cm.
Pushkin Museum, Moscow.

68. **A Boat on the Canal.**
Schoorldam, 1905.
Pen-and-ink and water-colour on paper,
12.5 × 18.5 cm.
Musée Picasso, Paris.

69. **Boy with a Pipe.**
Paris, 1905.
Oil on canvas, 100 × 81.3 cm.
Mr. and Mrs. John Hay Whitney Collection,
New York.

70. **Woman with a Fan.**
Paris, 1905.
Oil on canvas, 99 × 81.3 cm.
The National Gallery of Washington,
Donation of the W. Averell Harriman
Foundation.

71. **Boy and Horse.**
Paris, 1906.
Water-colour on paper pasted on wood,
50 × 32 cm.
The Tate Gallery, London.

72. **Sketch for "Arcady".**
Paris, spring 1906.
Pencil drawing, 29.2 × 44.5 cm.
Walter P. Chrysler Collection, New York.

73. **La Toilette.**
Gósol, spring-summer 1906.
Oil on canvas, 151 × 99 cm.
Albright-Knox Art Gallery, Buffalo.

74. **Fernande on a Mule.**
Gósol, spring-summer 1906.
Oil on wooden panel, 30 × 21 cm.
Heirs of the artist.

75. **Still Life with Drinking-Vessel.**
Gósol, spring-summer 1906.
Oil on canvas, 38.5 × 56 cm.
Hermitage Museum, Leningrad.

76. **The Woman with the Loaves.**
Gósol, spring-summer 1906.
Oil on canvas, 100 × 69.8 cm.
The Philadelphia Museum of Art,
Charles E. Ingersoll Donation.

77. **Fernande with a Kerchief on Her
Head.**
Gósol, spring-summer 1906.
Charcoal and gouache on paper, 66 × 49.5 cm.
Virginia Museum of Fine Arts, T. Catesby
Jones Collection.

78. **Young Gósol Man Wearing
Catalan Cap.**
Gósol, spring-summer 1906.
Gouache and water-colour on paper,
61.5 × 48 cm.
Göteborgs Kunstmuseum, Göteborg.

79. **Large Standing Nude.**
Gósol, spring-summer 1906.
Oil on canvas, 153 × 94 cm.
Mr. and Mrs. William Paley Collection,
New York.

80. **Portrait of Gertrude Stein.**
Paris, spring-summer 1906.
Oil on canvas, 100 × 81.3 cm.
The Metropolitan Museum of Art,
New York. Gertrude Stein Bequest.

81. **Self-portrait with a Palette
in His Hand.**
Paris, summer-autumn 1906.
Oil on canvas, 92 × 73 cm.
The Philadelphia Museum of Art,
E. A. Gallatin Collection.

82. **Study for "Two Women Arm
in Arm".**
Paris, summer-autumn 1906.
Water-colour and ink on paper,
21.2 × 13.5 cm.
Herbert Liesenfeld Collection, Düsseldorf.

83. **Head in Half-profile from the Left.**
Paris, autumn 1906.
Oil on canvas, 27 × 19 cm.
Heirs of the artist.

84. **Two Female Nudes.**
Paris, autumn-winter 1906.
Oil on canvas, 151.3 × 93 cm.
The Museum of Modern Art, New York.

85. **Bust of a Woman with
Her Eyes Closed.**
Paris, spring 1907.
Oil on canvas, 61 × 46 cm.
Hermitage Museum, Leningrad.

86. **Bust of a Woman in Half-profile
from the Left.**
Paris, spring-summer 1907.
Oil on canvas, 81 × 60 cm.
Berggruen Collection, Paris.

87. **One of the "Demoiselles".**
Paris, spring-summer 1907.
Oil on canvas, 119 × 93 cm.
Beyeler Collection, Basel.

88. **Bust of a "Demoiselle".**
Paris, summer 1907.
Oil on canvas, 65 × 58 cm.
Musée National d'Art Moderne, Paris.

89. **Les Demoiselles d'Avignon.**
Paris, spring-summer 1907.
Oil on canvas, 244 × 233.7 cm.
The Museum of Modern Art, New York.

90. **Landscape with Two Figures.**
Paris?, summer 1908.
Oil on canvas, 58 × 72 cm.
Musée Picasso, Paris.

91. **Bather.**
Paris, winter 1908-1909.
Oil on canvas, 130 × 97 cm.
Mrs. Bertram Smith Collection, New York.

92. **Bread and Fruit-Dish on a Table.**
Paris, early 1909.
Oil on canvas, 164 × 132.5 cm.
Kunstmuseum, Basel.

93. **Portrait of Fernande.**
Horta de Sant Joan, summer 1909.
Oil on canvas, 61 × 42 cm.
Kunstsammlung Nordheim-Westfalen,
Düsseldorf.

94. **The Pond in Horta.**
Horta de Sant Joan, summer 1909.
Oil on canvas, 81 × 65 cm.
Private collection, Paris.

95. **Girl with a Mandoline.**
Paris, early 1910.
Oil on canvas, 100.3 × 73.6 cm.
The Museum of Modern Art, New York.
Nelson A. Rockefeller Bequest.

96. **The Guitarist.**
Cadaqués, summer 1910.
Oil on canvas, 100 × 73 cm.
Musée National d'Art Moderne, Paris.

97. **Portrait of Daniel-Henry
Kahnweiler.**
Paris, autumn 1910.
Oil on canvas, 100.6 × 72.8 cm.
The Art Institute of Chicago.
Gift of Mrs. Gilbert W. Chapman.

98. **Landscape near Céret.**
Céret, summer 1911.
Oil on canvas, 65 × 50 cm.
The Solomon R. Guggenheim Museum,
New York.

99. **Guitar.**
Paris, early 1912.
Sheet metal and wire, 77.5 × 35 × 19.3 cm.
The Museum of Modern Art, New York.

100. **The Violin** (Jolie Eva).
Céret, spring 1912.
Oil on canvas, 81×60 cm.
Staatsgalerie, Stuttgart.

101. **Still Life with Chair Caning.**
Paris, May 1912.
Collage of oil, oilcloth, and paper on canvas
(oval), surrounded with rope, 27×35 cm.
Musée Picasso, Paris.

102. **The Scallop Shell** (Notre Avenir
est dans l'air).
Paris, spring 1912.
Oil on canvas (oval), 38×55.2 cm.
Mr. and Mrs. Leigh B. Block Collection,
Chicago.

103. **Bottle of Vieux Marc, Glass
and Newspaper.**
Céret, spring 1913.
Charcoal and pasted paper, 62.5×47 cm.
Musée National d'Art Moderne, Paris.

104. **Guitar.**
Céret, spring 1913.
Charcoal, pencil, ink and pasted paper,
66.3×49.5 cm.
The Museum of Modern Art, New York.
Nelson A. Rockefeller Bequest.

105. **Head.**
Paris or Céret, early 1913.
Charcoal and pasted paper on cardboard,
41×32 cm.
Private collection, London.

106. **Woman in an Armchair.**
Paris, autumn 1913.
Oil on canvas, 148×99 cm.
Mr. and Mrs. Victor W. Ganz Collection,
New York.

107. **Portrait of a Young Girl.**
Avignon, summer 1914.
Oil on canvas, 130×97 cm.
Musée National d'Art Moderne, Paris.

108. **Harlequin.**
Paris, late 1915.
Oil on canvas, 183.5×105.1 cm.
The Museum of Modern Art, New York.

109. **Manola with Pointilliste Technique.**
Barcelona, 1917.
Oil on canvas, 118×89 cm.
Picasso Museum, Barcelona.

110. **The Barcelona Harlequin.**
Barcelona, 1917.
Oil on canvas, 116×90 cm.
Picasso Museum, Barcelona.

111. **Bathers.**
Biarritz, summer 1918.
Oil on canvas, 26.3×21.7 cm.
Musée Picasso, Paris.

112. **Sleeping Peasants.**
Paris, 1919.
Gouache, water-colour and pencil,
31.1×48.9 cm.
The Museum of Modern Art, New York.

113. **Seated Woman.**
Paris, 1920.
Oil on canvas, 92×65 cm.
Musée Picasso, Paris.

114. **Three Musicians.**
Fontainebleau, summer 1921.
Oil on canvas, 200.7×222.9 cm.
The Museum of Modern Art, New York.

115. **Portrait of Igor Stravinsky.**
Paris, 24 May 1920.
Pencil on grey paper, 62×48.5 cm.
Musée Picasso, Paris.

116. **Three Women at the Spring.**
Fontainebleau, summer 1921.
Oil on canvas, 203.9×174 cm.
The Museum of Modern Art, New York.

117. **Harlequin** (Portrait of the painter
Jacint Salvadó).
Paris, 1923.
Oil on canvas, 130×97 cm.
Musée National d'Art Moderne, Paris.

118. **Paulo as Harlequin.**
Paris, 1924.
Oil on canvas, 130×97.5 cm.
Musée Picasso, Paris.

119. **Wineglass and Packet of
Cigarettes.**
Paris, 1924.
Oil on canvas, 16×22 cm.
Picasso Museum, Barcelona.

120. **Studio with Plaster Head.**
Juan-les-Pins (Provence), summer 1925.
Oil on canvas, 98.1×131.2 cm.
The Museum of Modern Art, New York.

121. **The Dance.**
Paris, June 1925.
Oil on canvas, 215×142 cm.
The Tate Gallery, London.

122. **Wire Construction** (model for the
monument to Guillaume Apollinaire).
Paris, late 1928.
Metal wire, 50.5×40.8×18.5 cm.
Musée Picasso, Paris.

123. **The Studio.**
Paris, winter 1927-1928.
Oil on canvas, 149.9×231.2 cm.
The Museum of Modern Art, New York,
Walter P. Chrysler, Jr. Donation.

124. **Girl before a Mirror.**
Boisgeloup, 14 March 1932.
Oil on canvas, 162.3×130.2 cm.
The Museum of Modern Art, New York,
Mrs. Simon Guggenheim Donation.

125. **Bather with Beach Ball.**
Boisgeloup, 30 August 1932.
Oil on canvas, 146.2×114.6 cm.
Private collection, New York.

126. **Guernica.**
Paris, 1 May - 4 June 1937.
Oil on canvas, 349.3×776.6 cm.
On loan to The Museum of Modern Art,
New York.

127. **Head of a Woman Weeping.**
Paris, 24 May 1937.
Pencil drawing on paper, 29×23 cm.

128. **Weeping Woman.**
Paris, 26 October 1937.
Oil on canvas, 60×49 cm.
Private collection, England.

129. **Women at Their Toilette**
(Cartoon for a tapestry).
Paris, spring 1938.
Oil and pasted paper on canvas,
299×448 cm.
Musée Picasso, Paris.

130. **Woman Dressing Her Hair.**
Royan, June 1940.
Oil on canvas, 130×97 cm.
Mrs. Bertram Smith Collection, New York.

131. **Stylized Woman's Head on
a Black Background.**
November 1945.
Lithograph, 32.5×25 cm.

132. **Bull.**
December 1945.
Lithograph, 1st state, 33.5×51.5 cm.

133. **Man with Sheep.**
Paris, 1944.
Bronze, 220×78×72 cm.
The Philadelphia Museum of Art, Donation
of R. Sturgis and Marion B. F. Ingersoll.

134. **Bull.**
Vallauris, 1947.
Ceramics
Ochre earth ground, 37×23×37 cm.
Musée Picasso, Antibes (France).

135. **Plate.**
12 April 1948.
Ceramic
Face painted in relief on rough surface,
31×37 cm.

136. **Square Plate.**
29 October 1947.
Ceramic
Face painted in relief on blue ground,
38.5×31 cm.
Musée Picasso, Antibes (France).

137. **Plate.**
1947.
Ceramic
Painted face, 32×38 cm.

138. **The Studio in Cannes.**
Cannes, 30 March 1956.
Oil on canvas, 114×146 cm.
Musée Picasso, Paris.

139. **The Maids of Honour** (Ensemble).
Cannes, 4 September 1957.
Oil on canvas, 46×37.5 cm.
Picasso Museum, Barcelona.

140. **The Maids of Honour.**
(Infanta Margarita María).
Cannes, 28 August 1957.
Oil on canvas, 18×14 cm.
Picasso Museum, Barcelona.

141. **The Maids of Honour.**
(Ensemble, without Velázquez or
Mari-Bárbola).
Cannes, 17 November 1957.
Oil on canvas, 35×27 cm.
Picasso Museum, Barcelona.

142. **The Maids of Honour**
(The doves, 1).
Cannes, 6 September 1957.
Oil on canvas, 80×100 cm.
Picasso Museum, Barcelona.

143. **The Maids of Honour**
(The doves, 5).
Cannes, 7 September 1957.
Oil on canvas, 100×80 cm.
Picasso Museum, Barcelona.

144. **The Maids of Honour**
(Isabel de Velasco).
Cannes, 30 December 1957.
Oil on canvas, 33×24 cm.
Picasso Museum, Barcelona.

145. **Bust of Woman Wearing a Hat.**
1962.
Coloured linocut, 63.5×52.5 cm.
Picasso Museum, Barcelona.

146. **Luncheon on the Grass**
(Le déjeuner sur l'herbe), after Manet.
Vauvenargues, March-August 1960.
Oil on canvas, 129×195 cm.
Musée Picasso, Paris.

147. **Aquatint.**
Mougins, 25 May 1968.
Plate 111 of the Series 347, 23.5×33 cm.

148. **Man's Head.**
Mougins, 9 July 1971.
Oil on canvas, 81×65 cm.

149. **Character.**
Mougins, 19 January 1972.
Oil on canvas, 100×81 cm.

150. **Man's Head.**
Mougins, 30 April 1972.
Oil on canvas, 81×65 cm.